The Economics of
CHARITY

The Economics of CHARITY

Essays on
the Comparative Economics and Ethics
of Giving and Selling, with Applications to Blood

PART I

ARMEN A. ALCHIAN and WILLIAM R. ALLEN
GORDON TULLOCK ANTHONY J. CULYER
THOMAS R. IRELAND DAVID B. JOHNSON

PART II

MICHAEL H. COOPER and ANTHONY J. CULYER
THOMAS R. IRELAND and JAMES V. KOCH
DAVID B. JOHNSON
MARILYN J. IRELAND A. J. SALSBURY

Published by

THE INSTITUTE OF ECONOMIC AFFAIRS
1973

First published in 1973
by
THE INSTITUTE OF ECONOMIC AFFAIRS

SBN 255 36046–0

Printed in Great Britain
by Unwin Brothers Limited
The Gresham Press, Old Woking, Surrey, England
A member of the Staples Printing Group

Preface

The *IEA Readings* are intended to assemble varying approaches to a subject by economists with complementary or contrasting expertise. This *Readings* assembles essays analysing the economics of 'giving' in Part I and discussions of its application to a commodity rarely discussed by economists (or other social scientists), blood, in Part II.

Readings No. 12 has evolved from a *Hobart Paper* (No. 41) in 1968 by two young economists, M. H. Cooper and A. J. Culyer, then both at the University of Exeter, entitled *The Price of Blood.* Its origin was a case of a shortage of blood which led to the question whether the British system of voluntary giving by blood donors was sufficient to ensure the supply of blood that could be made available for saving life. Point was given to the inquiry by the view of a distinguished and influential social administrator, the late Professor R. M. Titmuss, that there was no shortage of blood in Britain.[1] Messrs Cooper and Culyer concluded their analysis with the view that there might be a case for supplementing the voluntary donor system by pricing in one of varying forms.

In 1971 the Cooper/Culyer thesis was contested in a book by Titmuss, *The Gift Relationship*, which received widespread attention and acclaim. In it he widened the discussion to the economics and ethics of giving in general and the efficiency with which blood was given or sold in several countries, but mainly in the USA. His main conclusion on the general question was, in broadly ethical terms possibly over-simplified but essentially valid, that giving was good and selling was selfish or sordid, and on the particular application that selling blood had led to undesirable consequences, especially in the USA.

The Gift Relationship was accorded extensive reviews and broad approbation by academics and by the general press, at least for its moral flavour and fervour. Mr Edmund Leach, Master of King's College, Cambridge, for example, despite some reservations about the philosophical reasoning, praised the central Titmuss effort highly;[2] and the *Sunday Times* gave it ample coverage. (It has now

[1] *Choice and 'the Welfare State'*, Fabian Tract 370, 1967, reprinted in *Commitment to Welfare*, Allen and Unwin, 1968.

[2] 'The heart of the matter', *New Society*, 21 January, 1971.

also been published by Penguin Books.) More recent reflection by economists has produced more critical appraisal. Professors Simon Rottenburg[3] and Kenneth Arrow[4] have published major criticisms of the Titmuss analysis, the latter with praise for his stimulus to the discussion; and Professor Nathan Glazer,[5] in sympathetic vein, was also doubtful about much of the reasoning.

Although it is difficult to separate the economics of giving from the ethics in some of the discussion, it is of central importance for economists. This *Readings* suggest four inferences. The first is that it is over-simple to distinguish between giving as good and selling as not good. Professors Armen A. Alchian and William R. Allen, authors of perhaps the most penetrating introductory economics textbook for students in the English language,[6] outline elements in the pure theory of giving in an extract, slightly revised and anglicised, from their book. It shows that philanthropy does not conflict with economic theory, which can be applied to giving as well to selling. Professor Gordon Tullock, in a characteristically debonair and incisive discussion of 'The Charity of the Uncharitable', analyses the less evident motives for giving. Mr Anthony J. Culyer, a rising young economist at the University of York and author of a new work on social policy,[7] inquires searchingly into the meaning of the concepts used by economists and sociologists and concludes with new insights. And Professors Thomas R. Ireland and David B. Johnson, young American economists who have worked together to develop the theory of philanthropy, review the outlines of their thinking and findings.

These five essays offer an attempt to analyse the economics of giving, and they emerge with conclusions more refined and less apparent than is common in everyday thinking and some sociological writing. Giving is not to be separated easily into a category on a higher moral plane than selling: much depends on the terms, the timing, and the spirit; selling is normally part of a process of exchange in which both parties benefit; giving can create a sense of indebted-

3 'The Production and Exchange of Used Body Parts', in *Toward Liberty: Essays in honour of Ludwig von Mises*, Vol. II, Institute for Humane Studies, Menlo Park, California, 1971.

4 'Gifts and Exchanges', in *Philosophy and Public Affairs*, Princeton University Press, Summer 1972.

5 'Blood', in *The Public Interest*, Summer 1971.

6 *University Economics*, Wadsworth Publishing Company, Belmont, California, 1972 (3rd edn.); in the UK, Prentice-Hall International, Hemel Hempstead, Herts.

7 *The Economics of Social Policy*, Martin Robertson, London, 1973.

ness in the recipient,[8] and it can create and foment an attitude of dependence.[9] In particular collective giving, as in the Welfare State or in aid to other countries,[10] can do short-term good at the expense of long-term harm by weakening the capacity and the will to build independence. Much of the economics of giving has been developed in the USA: hence most of the authors in Part I are American economists who are showing that economics can be applied to maximise the utility of giving no less than that of selling.

Second, if the obscurantist distinction between giving and selling can be removed from the discussion, it is possible to consider, as Messrs. Cooper and Culyer argued in 1968 and amplify persuasively in a new essay in Part II, how far and in what form methods of payment or 'compensation' can be added to voluntary giving to expand the supply of blood to save life. This approach is reinforced by two shorter discussions: in the first, a joint essay, Professors Ireland and James Koch attempt a hypothetical supply curve of blood with a range of prices; in the second, Professor Johnson contrasts and criticises the British and American methods of assembling volunteer and paid blood.

Third, the Titmuss argument was that blood provided at a price by 'professional' blood suppliers created a larger risk of infection than did blood given by voluntary donors. This charge raised technical issues beyond the competence of economists, and a British doctor and an American lawyer were invited to contribute essays on these aspects to a special section, 'Technical Evidence'. If there were no method of testing blood for infection, the proposition would weaken the case for generating supplies by payment. But there appear to be technical developments in testing blood which reduce or remove the risk: the authoritative medical contribution by Dr A. J. Salsbury in England and the incisive legal essay by Professor Marilyn J. Ireland of the USA suggest that the Titmuss hypothesis may be partly or wholly refuted. In that event, the medical/legal (as distinct

---

[8] Professor Thomas Szasz has argued that paying gives the power to reject undesired medical treatment. (BBC broadcast, 2 October, 1972.)

[9] The late F. A. Harper (Institute for Humane Studies, California) once quoted a paraphrase of a saying by the Talmudic scholar Moses Maimonides:

'The noblest charity is to prevent a man from accepting charity, and the best alms are to show and enable a man to dispense with alms.'

[10] P. T. Bauer, 'Foreign Aid: an Instrument for Progress?', in Barbara Ward and P. T. Bauer, *Two Views on Aid to Developing Countries*, Occasional Paper 9, IEA, 1966, and *Dissent on Development*, Weidenfeld and Nicolson, 1971.

from the theoretical/ethical) reason for distinguishing between volunteer and paid blood may be removed.

Fourth, the implication that a society which makes use of markets and pricing is in a sense more materialistic and less humane than one that does not appears questionable. Professor David Johnson's essay analyses three kinds of markets: the private market, for long the staple of economic analysis, the political market, made familiar in the past decade by the writings of Professors J. M. Buchanan and Gordon Tullock and other economists in America, and the charity market, the newest addition, in which economists analyse the economics of giving and receiving in much the same way as they have long analysed the economics of buying and selling. Professors Thomas Ireland and Johnson have done much to develop the economics of charity by working on the foundations laid by Buchanan and Tullock and others in America.

The Keynesian concentration on the macro-economics of national totals—income, expenditure, production, wages, costs and other aggregates and their derivatives—in large part explains the relative neglect of the potential use of markets and pricing techniques in solving economic problems. It is perhaps because the study of markets has continued to interest economists more in the USA than in Britain that the fruitful developments in the economics of giving and in the possible application of pricing to unfamiliar commodities or services have been more prominent there. In Britain the Institute has pioneered or furthered the application of pricing analysis not only to blood but also to water, fire-fighting services, refuse collection, animal semen, telephones, broadcasting, roads, car parking, and, not least, welfare services, many or most of which are neglected by economists reared in the macro-economic influence and tradition.

This *Readings* introduces new economic thinking to British readers and takes further its application to the possible use of pricing for increasing the supply of blood. Assembling material from ten authors, some of whom were preoccupied with other work, has delayed publication; some of the contributions, notably those by Messrs Cooper and Culyer, were first written in 1971 (revised before publication). The collection will be of interest primarily to teachers and students of economics but also to sociologists, social administrators and others concerned with the economics and ethics of giving in general and to surgeons, physicians and others anxious about the shortage of blood. The constitution of the Institute requires it to dissociate its Trustees, Directors and

Advisers from the analyses and conclusions of its authors, but it offers this *Readings* as an illustration of the potency of market analysis in an activity not normally thought to be the province of the economist: the analysis of the charity market in general and of an unfamiliar potential market in particular.

August 1973

EDITOR

Contents

PART I
Principles: Giving

1. The Pure Economics of Giving*

ARMEN A. ALCHIAN

and

WILLIAM R. ALLEN

Professors of Economics, University of California, Los Angeles

THE AUTHORS

ARMEN A. ALCHIAN is Professor of Economics at the University of California, Los Angeles. He is a member of the IEA's Advisory Council. His publications include works on inflation, costs, investment criteria, property rights and formal economic theory.

WILLIAM R. ALLEN is Professor of Economics at the University of California, Los Angeles.

I. THE UTILITY OF GIVING

Charity or philanthropy totals to billions of dollars annually. Charitable foundations and colleges are two prime examples—not to mention religious groups and individual gifts. Musical concerts, museums, libraries, and art galleries are open to the public at prices far below those that would clear the market, precisely because the sponsor wants to be charitable. The Ford, Gulbenkian, Mellon, and Rockefeller Foundations, to name but a few of the largest, are supposed to give wealth—not sell it. Almost every university provides services at less than costs, because they are supported by people who want to give educational opportunities to (*smart*) young people. In all these cases of charity, because the price is zero, a long list of applicants must be screened on some other competitive, discriminatory basis. How do the results differ from those of market-price competition? Economic analysis will shed light on that question—perhaps with some surprises.

The *economics* of charity or gifts may seem contradictory. If, according to economic theory, people seek to increase their utility, how then can they give gifts? Are these acts to be set aside from economics as unexplainable behaviour? Not at all. I may believe that other people should consume certain goods, and I may so value their doing so that I am prepared to pay. Thus I pay to have milk and food for my children. I may so value other people's reading of good literature that I am willing to pay to make it available to them. For this kind of situation, we see people engaging in charity or philanthropy.

The postulates of economic theory do not say that man is concerned only about himself. He can be concerned about other people's situations also.

From my point of view, I would rather you were richer than poorer, even if it cost me something. It is even possible that a £1 decrease in my wealth could reduce my utility by *less* than a £1 increase in *your* wealth would increase *my* utility. Then I would contribute wealth to you. The likelihood of this happening is stronger if my wealth is large and yours is small. And that is a refutable proposition. As my wealth increases relative to yours, my willingness to contribute to you will increase just as an increasing amount of sweets increases my willingness to give up sweets for ice cream. Furthermore, a *matching grant* would induce me to give still more, because now I know that each pound I give up gets you more than £1. This implies that matching grants should be commonly observed in charity. And they are.[1]

II. THE ECONOMIC ANALYSIS OF GIVING

Who gains what from a gift?

A gift (unintentional or intentional) can be defined as an allocation at a price below the open-market price by those 'giving away' the goods. Suppose I own a house that would rent for £100 monthly in the open market; however, I offer it to you for only £40 as a favour. Suppose you would have been prepared to pay £80 for this house. We now have three valuations: *A*—the market rent of the house (£100), *B*—the price at which you *would* have been willing to rent the house (£80), and *D*—the price of the house to you (£40). We want one more item of information: How much would you have spent on housing if I had not made you this special offer? Your answer we shall suppose to be £65, denoted by *C*; that is, you would have chosen a smaller or inferior house if I had not offered you the £100 one for £40. The following new concepts can now be specified. The difference between *A* and *D* (i.e., $A - D$) is the total wealth transferred *from* me, the donor. The house is worth £100, and I get only £40 for it. In this transfer of £60 of wealth from me, what did you get?

First, compare what you did pay, £40, with what you would have paid for some house (£65) had I not provided you with this unusual opportunity. This difference ($C - D$) is (£65 − £40) £25, a measure of how much *money* you can henceforth release every month from housing purchases and use in any way you like. Call this an increase in your 'money' wealth, a gift of £25 to you. The quantity ($C - D$) *could* be negative, indicating that the recipient would spend more on this kind of good if the subsidy had not been offered.

Second, compare the housing expenditure you would have made had this special offer not been available with what the house I made available is worth to *you*. This difference ($B - C$) is, in our example, £80 − £65 = £15. You now have £15 more of wealth in the *specific* form of housing than you otherwise would have had.

Of my £60 wealth transfer, we have accounted for £40: £25 ($C - D$) as a *general* (money) wealth increase to you and £15 ($B - C$) more to you of a *specific* resource, housing; that leaves £20

1 Income-tax reductions for gifts are another way to reduce the donor's costs of giving money to other people—by making other taxpayers pay more to offset my reduced tax payments.

($A - B$) unaccounted for. As far as *you* are concerned, that extra £20 is simply wasted: you have acquired for £40 a £100 house that you value at only £80. Although I have borne a cost of £60, the gift is worth only £40 to you. From your point of view, if I had given you £60 in money to spend as you wished, you would have been better off by £20. This 'waste' (from your point of view) of £20 is the third component of the £60 gift.

Do not forget *my* (the donor's) point of view. Is there a waste of £20? If I am fully aware of these implications, and nevertheless choose to make the particular gift that I do, then from my point of view it is worth £60 to me to give you the gain of £25 in cash and £15 in superior housing. It is worth more than £20 to *me* to induce you to live in a house that costs £100 (but which you think is worth only £80). I have put you in an environment that I prefer for you.

For *every* instance in which goods are transferred (from me to you) at less than the free-market exchange-equilibrium price, we can summarise the analysis succinctly if we let

A be the market value of the transferred goods;
B the hypothetical price which, if existing, would have induced you to buy the goods;
C the money you would have paid for whatever amount of the transferred good you otherwise would have purchased;
D the amount actually paid by you.

Then,

($A - D$) is the net total cost to me of the resources transferred to you which can be subdivided into the following three components:
($A - B$) is the waste, from your (the receiver's) point of view, but not necessarily from mine (the giver's);
($B - C$) is the value to *you* of the extra specific resources made available to you.
($C - D$) is the general-purchasing-power wealth transfer to you.

But there is more to consider. We must not ignore the impact that opportunities to capture subsidies or gifts will have on the behaviour of potential receivers in their attempts to qualify for the subsidies. Prospects of competitive applicants can be improved if they spend money or revise their activities so as to reach a more advantageous position, as determined by the allocative criteria used by the donor. Each applicant will be induced to spend an amount, at the most, equal to the expected value of the subsidy (as valued by the potential recipient). This is an extra cost not included in the prior concepts—and sometimes an important source of livelihood for those who can help applicants qualify for these gifts. Examples are lawyers, public relations experts and politicians.

III. APPLICATIONS OF THE ANALYSIS

Business dinner dance for employees

To illustrate the consequences of a gift, let us apply the analysis to an employees' dinner dance sponsored by a business firm. Suppose the cost of the dinner is £14 per person, but the company sells tickets to employees for only £6. Question: Who gets what by this company gift? The quantity A is £14, the market value or cost of the service being sold for £6, which is denoted D (using the letters in the earlier example). We now consider several alternatively circumstanced employees.

Employee I would have spent £14 on a dinner dance anyway, even without this subsidy. His C is £14. If he were willing to buy this particular dinner-dance ticket even if the price had been the full £14, his B is also £14. Now we can carry through the computations. The company spends £8 per ticket as a subsidy $(A - D) = (£14 - £6) = £8$. Employee I gets a cash gain of £8, $(C - D) = (£14 - £6) = £8$. His gain in *specific kind* of goods is zero, for $(B - C) = £14 - £14 = 0$. From his point of view there is no waste, for $(A - C) = £14 - £14 = 0$. The subsidy has given him simply a cash release of the full amount of the £8 subsidy, to spend however he wishes.

Consider employee II, who does less dinner dancing and would have spent only £7 for dinner dancing in the absence of this particular party. His C is £7. Suppose further that he would have been willing to pay £9 for this particularly elaborate party if the price had been that high, but he would have refused this particular party if the price were higher. His B is £9. For him, $C - D = (£7 - £6) = £1$; he gets £1 cash gain. His $(B - C) = (£9 - £7) = £2$, which means he gets £2 more of dinner dancing (as he values it) than he otherwise would. And the component $(A - B) = £14 - £9 = £5$ is a measure of the waste of company money. The company spent £14 for something worth only £9 to *him*. Of the total £8 net cost to the company, £5 was a waste and £2 gave employee II more dinner dancing than he otherwise would have had, and £1 was his cash gain.

And then there is employee III, who does not think the dinner dance is worth even £6. He buys no ticket and gets no gain of any kind.

Question: If you were the owner of the company, what would you think of partially subsidised dinner dances as a scheme to aid the employees to have a good time? Which employees?

Reconsider employee II, who would have paid £9 for a dinner-dance ticket. Why does he not play it smart? Why does he not buy a ticket for £6 and sell it to some outsider for £14, thereby gaining £8? This is better for him than the alternative gain of £1 in money and £2 more of dinner-dance activity. But the company prohibits him from doing so, probably because the managers do not want outsiders at the dance. Then why does not our employee resell the ticket to some other employee? There are two cases to consider. On the one hand, the supply of tickets at £6 may be large enough to provide all that the employees want at that price. But if the supply of tickets is not large enough to accommodate all demanders at £6, the lucky employees who first get tickets could resell them at a higher price and take their gift entirely as generalised money gains, rather than as less-valued dinner-dance activity. Permitting resale is to break the connection between dinner dancing and gifts, allowing some gift to those who do not dinner dance.

To make this analysis strike home, inquire if at your place of employment some have special parking rights not granted to others. If so, apply the above analysis to discern who gains what as compared to selling the parking rights.

Foreign aid

The United States government grants aid (gifts) to some foreign governments, ostensibly for specific purposes. If the US government gives $10 million to the Egyptian government to build a dam, what has Egypt gained? What would the Egyptians have done without the gift of aid? Suppose they intended to build the dam anyway, financing it by domestic saving. To that extent, a gift for the dam releases wealth of the Egyptian government for other things. The gift purportedly 'for a dam' is actually for general purposes—the Egyptian government now simply has $10 million more than it otherwise would have. Conceivably it could lower taxes—thus giving the Egyptians that much more income for general consumption—or the government itself will spend the extra funds.

Why, then, give the money 'for a dam'? One possible answer is that otherwise they would not have built the dam, so that the gift does provide one more dam. The embarrassing implication of this answer is that this use of the money for the dam is so unproductive that the Egyptian government itself would not have paid for the dam. Or, if they were too poor to have done so, a simple gift of $10 million to the Egyptians with no strings on its use would have enabled the Egyptians themselves to decide what were the most valuable uses of the extra wealth made available. Of course, government officials of both the United States and Egypt understand all this, and the 'conditional' form of the grant is employed primarily to try to induce the Egyptian government to behave more in accord with the US government's view of Egypt's interest.

Free school transportation

Children in state schools are given free bus rides to school. From this gift (subsidy) of bus rides to school children, who gains what? The answer should now be easy. The parents of the children must be classed according to those who would have provided transportation for their children and those who would have made their children walk. The first group receive all the subsidy as a general increase in their wealth. They can buy more of all things with the wealth which otherwise would have paid for their children's transportation. The other parents get no gain in general wealth, but take it all in the specific form of better transportation for the children. 'Free bus rides' for school children turn out then to be composites of gifts of wealth to parents and of better transportation for children, with some families getting all of it in general wealth, some in mixtures, and some exclusively in more transportation.

The corollary of our general proposition is that gifts might as well be resaleable or given as money by the donors to the extent that the recipients already possess or use the services or resources given to them. If I am given a case of beer each month by some kind-hearted person who thinks he is inducing me to drink more beer, he should note that my family already consumes a case a month. Therefore, I shall temporarily stop buying beer and use the released wealth for other purposes. Whether he gives beer (whether or not he lets me sell it) or money is essentially irrelevant.

IV. UNINTENTIONAL CHARITY

Intentional and unintentional gifts cannot always be distinguished.

Nor, as we shall see, can we conclude that every allocation of resources made at less than a market-clearing price, even at a price as low as zero, involves a gain to the recipient.

TV station franchises

Currently, anyone wanting to operate a new television station in the United States must first obtain permission of the Federal Communications Commission (FCC). Rights to operate a station are valuable, and many applicants appeal to the FCC for authorisation.[2] Each will try to show why he is the proper person. How? In sales of government-owned forests and oil lands, the 'right' person is the one who will bid the most, with the proceeds going to the public treasuries. But the law creating the FCC forbids it to allocate channels on the basis of competitive money bids. Nor is 'first come, first served' the rule (although it was for radio in the early 1920s). Instead, the commission in some unspecified manner chooses among applicants.

The applicant is asked to show why the community 'needs' another station—over protestations of the existing station owner, whose television station's value would fall. Because there is no money-price competition of the open-market-place variety, other competition in terms of applicants' attributes takes on more significance. Money that would have been paid to the government under price competition for that right or 'property' will instead be devoted, at least in part, to competition for the commissioners' support. Since something worth millions is at stake, millions are spent seeking the licence.

Criteria of selection

On what criteria do commissioners select the winner? That is what the various applicants would like to know. They do know that the applicant should be a man of respectability, good moral standing, public service, and high education. A newspaper publisher or a radio-station operator has an advantage, for he is experienced in news collecting and dissemination. If he does not put on religious programmes, if he plays only jazz and Western shows and intends to present few if any 'cultural' programmes, he will lose competitive rank. He must detect the preferences, tastes, and kinds of shows that

[2] The number of channels that could be used at one time is not a technologically fixed constant. It depends upon the kind of receiving and transmitting equipment. With more expensive and sensitive receivers and transmitters, the number of available channels could be increased considerably. And the possibilities with cable are enormous.

commissioners think the public ought to be shown; then he must suggest that he will present those programmes. He must be careful not to offer explicit, detectable bribes to the commissioners. On the other hand, if in the past he hired some of the FCC technical staff to operate his other radio or television stations, of if he is an ex-Congressman, or if he employs an ex-Congressman as a legal counsel to advocate his case to the FCC, this indicates that he recognises able people, and he therefore could successfully operate a television station. All the value of the rights to broadcast accrues neither to the federal taxpayers nor to the winning applicant; instead, part is consumed in legal fees, costs of publicity, production of kinds of programmes the FCC prefers, and other expenses to win the licence. Thus, even though the nominal price of the licence is zero, the costs of getting it are substantial—not to mention the costs of the losers' efforts.

The magnitude of the gift is revealed by the jump in the stock prices of companies that receive a licence. Fortunately for the station owners, this wealth gain *is* transferable: they can sell that station to other people instead of keeping the gift in the form of a television station. Was it the intention of the government to make a gift? The *motivation* of this rationing procedure is to 'safeguard' the public and to provide the public with what is 'good'. The preceding illustration does not imply that the Federal Communications Commission acts irresponsibly. The commissioners act just as anyone else would in the same situation.

More examples could be presented. Competitive prices are not used initially in the US to allocate licences to operate (a) scheduled passenger airplanes, (b) liquor stores (in many states), (c) taxis (most cities), (d) banks (most states), and (e) sugar beet and tobacco farms.[3] But these rights are saleable once they have been awarded. For example, the right to operate a taxi in New York City sells for about $25,000.

Non-transferable gifts

There is a class of possibly unintended gifts where the allocated goods *cannot* be reallocated or resold after they are initially allocated. Rights to enter university, obtain a medical training, enter the US or the UK, join some unions, adopt a child, play golf on a publicly-owned golf course, camp in a national park—these rights are often

3 Similar examples (including (a), (b) and (c)) could be given for the UK.

allocated at zero prices or at prices below those that would clear the market. (Consequently, there are 'shortages' and allocation by methods discussed in the earlier examples.) Whether or not the allocated item is subsequently resaleable does not destroy the fact of gift. However, that affects the extent to which the gift can be realised as an increase in the recipient's general wealth, instead of only as a gain in a particular kind of good. For example, when a municipally-owned golf course underprices its services and has a waiting list and 'shortage' of playing space, those 'lucky' enough to get access receive a particularised gain—if they have not had to pay other costs to get on the reservation list.

Nothing in economic analysis warrants a judgement about which allocative procedures are good or bad. That judgement must be based on criteria derived from other sources.

2. The Charity of the Uncharitable

GORDON TULLOCK

University Professor of Economics, Virginia Polytechnic Institute and State University

THE AUTHOR

GORDON TULLOCK was born in Rockford, Illinois, and educated there and at the University of Chicago, graduating from its law school in 1947 (after interruption for military service). From 1947 to 1956 he served in the US Foreign Service (he was vice-consul in Tientsin, China, when it was seized by the Communists in 1949). After spending 1958–59 as a Post Doctoral Fellow at the Thomas Jefferson Center for Political Economy, University of Virginia, he was appointed Assistant and later Associate Professor in the Department of International Studies at the University of South Carolina (1959–62); 1962–67 Associate Professor of Economics, University of Virginia; 1967–68 Professor of Economics and Political Science, Rice University. From 1968 to 1972 he was Professor of Economics and Public Choice at Virginia Polytechnic Institute and State University, and is now University Professor there.

Professor Tullock has been a member of the board and secretary of the Public Choice Society since its foundation, and is editor of *Public Choice*. Co-author with Professor James M. Buchanan of *The Calculus of Consent* (1962); his other books include *The Politics of Bureaucracy* (1965) and *Private Wants, Public Means* (1970). He has contributed widely to learned journals.

GLOSSARY

Log-rolling process—Trading of votes, either by politicians or by individual voters. For example, I vote for a law which I would rather not have because you promise to vote for a law that I want which you would normally vote against. It can occur only if my desire to get my way on the first issue is greater than on the second, and yours is greater on the second than on the first.

Monotonic—Always moving in the same direction, but not necessarily at the same rate.

Prisoner's dilemma—A situation discovered by game theorists in the early 1950s and apparently very widespread. The title 'prisoner's dilemma' comes from the example by which it was first explained. When the parties cannot make a binding contract between themselves, which is common in politics, they will each choose that optimum which is best, granted that they cannot control the other party's decision. The results are frequently much less pleasant for the parties than if they could make a binding contract.

Continuum—A dimension upon which something or other can be arranged, for example, a continuum of height from the shortest to the tallest.

I. INTRODUCTION

The common view among modern intellectuals is that income redistribution is considered to be a rather simple and almost entirely ethical matter. There are basically two theories. The first is that those of us who are well-off use the state as a mechanism for making gifts to the poor.[1] The second view, the 'Downsian',[2] is that in a democracy the poor are able to use their votes to obtain transfers from the rest of society. These two views are sometimes combined into the view that the bulk of the population takes money from the rich and gives it to the poor by the democratic process.

The two views sum up the standard justification for redistribution. Unfortunately, these essentially ethical approaches cannot explain the bulk of the redistribution that takes place in practice in most democracies. They explain a small amount of it, but most redistribution comes from other motives and achieves other ends. Since these two ideas are probably fairly firmly engrained in the mind of the reader, I should like to discuss the main facts of redistribution before I begin formal analysis.

First, the amount of redistribution the poor receive is, in part, a function of the extent to which they vote.[3] Thus, to at least some extent, the money they receive must represent their use of political power, rather than a charitable gift from the rest of society. Thus, the first of the explanations above cannot be the entire explanation.

Secondly, anybody examining the status of the poor in the modern world must realise that democracies do not make very large gifts to them. Messrs. A. L. Webb and J. E. B. Sieve carefully examined the statistics on income redistribution in Britain.[4] The basic objective

---

[1] This is well represented by James Rodgers and Harold Hochman in 'Pareto Optimal Redistribution', *American Economic Review*, September 1969, pp. 542–57. Hochman and Rodgers, of course, are much more sophisticated in their handling of the problem than I have indicated in this paragraph. Nevertheless, they espouse the point of view outlined above. Their article has attracted a large number of comments, many of which are markedly less sophisticated than the original work.

[2] A. Downs, *An Economic Theory of Democracy*, New York, 1957, especially pp. 198–201.

[3] B. R. Fry and R. F. Winters, 'The Politics of Redistribution', *American Political Science Review*, June 1970, pp. 508–22. For a discussion of the reasons why the poor exert less political influence than their *per capita* voting strength would appear to give them, Bruno Frey, 'Why Do High Income People Participate More in Politics?', *Public Choice*, Fall 1971, pp. 101–105.

[4] A. L. Webb and J. E. B. Sieve, *Income Redistribution and the Welfare State*, Occasional Papers on Social Administration No. 41, Bell, London, 1971.

was to scrutinise them for accuracy and possible improvement. Their conclusion on what the statistics show is:

'Compared with 1937, . . . there is good reason to assume the degree of inequality had not changed by 1959.[19] [[19]The overall change between 1959 and 1968 is also very small.] *Therefore, the estimated inequality of final incomes remained constant over a period of twenty years which saw the establishment and growth to some stability of the 'welfare state'*.

The overall changes between 1961 and 1969 amounted to an increase in the regressive effects of taxation, offset by a progressive change in the magnitude of benefits.'[5]

Since the basic data collected in Britain by J. L. Nicholson and analysed by Webb and Sieve were selected in such a way as to increase the redistributive effect of the Welfare State, this conclusion is particularly striking not because of bias on their part but because of statistical difficulties. Nevertheless,

'Considering only the more redistributive of the fiscal and social welfare systems, on the basis of a favourable selection of all welfare policies during a period widely acclaimed as egalitarian, we have seen that our society has remained fairly consistently unequal.'[6]

Granted the massive amounts of income transferred back and forth through the population by the British government, it is clear that the major *effect*, and probably the major *purpose*, of this transfer cannot be to help the poor.[7] With well in excess of 30 per cent of the average individual's received income taxed away in one way or another and the defence burden much lower as a part of GNP than it was in 1937, it is clear that there are massive resources available for aiding the poor if that was indeed the objective of the British government.

II. EXPLAINING REDISTRIBUTION

What has been done to explain redistribution in a democracy?[8]

---

[5] *Ibid.*, p. 109. This comment is particularly revealing since both Webb and Sieve are vigorous advocates of the British Welfare State and the subject matter of their book is the improvement of statistics on its effects.

[6] *Ibid.*, p. 116.

[7] Webb and Sieve would agree about the major effect, but not about the purpose. They appear to believe that the present transfer system in Britain is a badly designed—one might even say *pathologically* badly designed—effort to help the poor.

[8] This essay is entirely concerned with redistribution in democracies because that is where our knowledge of politics is best. I should not like to leave the implication that I think redistribution operates better in despotisms.

The first theory in recent time is the argument of Professor Anthony Downs that democracy will always lead to transfer of income from the wealthy to the poor. Indeed, he regards it as a major justification of democracy. We may contrast it with Professor Benjamin Ward's view that redistribution in democracy would be essentially indeterminate.[9] Finally, there is the view expressed in *The Calculus of Consent* that the nature of the voting process in democracy is such that real resources will be transferred away from the rich, although it is not specified who will receive them.[10] Naturally I espouse the third view, but the Ward theory will be used to supplement it by indicating that the recipients cannot be identified.[11]

The essence of the difference between the Downs and the Ward theories is simply that Downs implicitly assumes that redistribution must take place along a continuum in which people are arranged from the poorest to the wealthiest. At first glance, there would seem to be no obvious reason why the bottom 51 per cent of the population, using their majority to take money from the wealthy, would be a more likely outcome than the top 51 per cent using their majority to take money from the poor. Indeed, the 2 per cent of the population lying at the middle line would be the determining factor in such a choice, and hence we might anticipate that money would come from both ends to the middle.

By definition the wealthy have more money and hence can be subject to heavier taxes. Thus the cost of admitting a wealthy person into a coalition, which proposes to transfer money away from the 49 per cent of the population who are not members, is higher than the cost of permitting the entry of a poor person. One would therefore anticipate that voting coalitions would be made up in such a way as to minimise the number of wealthy members.[12] This is, indeed, the element of truth in the Downs model, is part of the Buchanan-

[9] B. Ward, 'Majority Rule and Allocation', *Journal of Conflict Resolution*, December 1961, pp. 379–89. Note that Ward actually demonstrates that there would be a cyclical majority in all such cases. Since the process must stop, however, and in observed reality *does* stop at some point, the statement that he proved indeterminancy of the process is not an unjust summary.

[10] J. M. Buchanan and G. Tullock, *The Calculus of Consent*, University of Michigan Press, Ann Arbor, 1962.

[11] The two models may be reconciled by use of the apparatus presented by Gordon Tullock in 'A Simple Algebraic Logrolling Model', *American Economic Review*, June 1970, pp. 419–26.

[12] W. Riker, *The Theory of Political Coalitions*, New Haven, 1962.

Tullock model, and must be admitted as a modification of the Ward model.

Dividing the spoils

If the dominant coalition is likely to be made up of the bottom 51 per cent of the population, this tells us nothing much about how it will divide the spoils. Further, it obviously must contain many who are not poor by any ordinary definition. If we accept the bottom 10 per cent of the population as poor, they make up only a fifth of this coalition of the bottom 51 per cent. If we are more generous and count 20 per cent of the population as poor, they make up two-fifths. Clearly this minority cannot dominate the coalition. If they received more per head than the other members of the coalition, they would do so because the lower middle-class was generous.

Coalition strategy

In formal bargaining theory, it is obvious that any transfer mechanism must provide at least as much for the top portion of this bottom 51 per cent coalition as for anyone else in the coalition. If it does not the 49 per cent who are not members can very readily purchase the top 2 per cent for a coalition that transfers a small amount from the top income groups to this small 2 per cent group and to no one else. Indeed, such a coalition might take the entire transfer out of the bottom part of the population instead of out of the top. The reasoning so far would indicate that the people toward the top of the bottom 51 per cent might receive much more than the people at the lower end. The only restriction on a delivery of the bulk of the resources transferred from the wealthy to the upper end of the bottom coalition (other than the charitable instincts at the upper end) would seem to be the possibility that the wealthy would attempt a coalition with the very poor.

In the real world, we see signs of such coalition attempts. Among people who argue that all transfers should be strictly limited to the very poor by a stringent means test, it is likely that wealthy persons predominate. This is, of course, sensible from even a selfish standpoint. They could arrange to give to the present-day poor considerably more money than they are now receiving, in return for a coalition in which transfers to people in the upper part of the bottom 51 per cent are terminated, and make a neat 'profit'. This particular coalition has so far foundered largely because of miscalculations by the poor. They realise that the interests of the wealthy are clearly not congruent with their interests, but they do *not* realise that the interests of the people between the 20th and the 51st percentile of the income distribution are also *not* identical with theirs. They therefore tend to favour a coalition with the less poor rather than with the wealthy.[13]

Thus, an organisation of society in which all transfers were made by a special electorate composed of people in the top 10 per cent of the income stream who tax themselves to benefit others might lead to larger transfers to the genuinely poor than they now receive in the electoral systems of the USA or the UK. Certainly, if we fixed the total amount transferred away from the upper income groups at its present level but gave them complete discretion on how it was to be spent, they would spend far more of it on the very poor.

Income transfers in reality

So far, however, we have unrealistically assumed that transfers must be made between different *income* groups along a continuum.* In the real world, we observe that the bulk of the transfers are made to groups *not* defined by income. Farmers, university students, older people and other 'welfare' beneficiaries *regardless of their income*, and,

---

[13] The situation is interesting and we may pause briefly to examine it by way of a three-person model. Suppose we have wealthy Mr *A*, middle-class Mr *B*, and poor Mr *C*. *B* and *C* form a coalition for the purpose of extracting money from *A*; let us begin by assuming that the money is equally divided between them. Suppose, then, that Mr *C*'s income is £1,000 per year before transfer, Mr *B*'s is £2,000 per year, and Mr *A*'s is £3,000 per year. *B* and *C* vote a tax of £500 on *A* which is equally divided between them. Clearly if this amount of transfer were somehow externally fixed at £500 but Mr *A* were permitted to decide how it was to be allocated, he would give all of it to Mr *C*. (Such a decision might be made available to taxpayers by allowing them to 'earmark' on their income tax returns a portion of their tax for alternative transfers.) He would reason that not until Mr *C*'s income had risen to £2,000 per year was it sensible to supplement Mr *B*'s income. Mr *B* receives his payment simply because he wants it, not because there is any charitable motive involved on the part of anyone.

Under the circumstances, it is clear that Mr *A* would be willing to enter into a coalition with Mr *C* under which a transfer of £300 was made from *A* to *C* and none was made to *B*. This would be to the advantage of Mr *C*, and it seems likely that only the generally bad information and low IQ and/or motivation which we observe among the poor prevents such coalitions. Indeed, it is possible the poor would do better if they depended entirely on the charitable motives of the wealthy. It might be that Mr *A*, if left entirely to himself, would be willing to give Mr *C* more than £250, although he objects to spending £500 for £250 apiece to *B* and *C*. Most people, after all, are to some extent charitable and it may well be that the very poor would do better than at present if they depended on the charity of the wealthy.

* Glossary, p. 16.

probably, the intellectual class are the main recipients of transfers, even though the bulk of these groups are not poor.[14]

If the real world is one in which transfers are made to organised groups, which receive their transfers largely in terms of their political power, there is no reason why we should anticipate that the poor would do particularly well. For one thing, they are hard to organise. Thus, the very large transfers that we do observe in the world are essentially demonstrations of the Ward proof (that transfers are indeterminate), supplemented by the Buchanan-Tullock log-rolling* process, which only accidentally benefit the bottom 10 to 15 per cent of the population. For the reasons above, we would anticipate that the top income groups would do rather badly from these transfers, and they do. The Nicholson figures show that the people in Britain whose income is £3,100 or more per year retain only about 67 per cent of their income after the transfers (both taxes and benefits) have been accomplished.[15] But we would anticipate that the beneficiaries of these transfers would not be particularly concentrated among the poor and, indeed, granted their general political ineptitude, one might expect that they would do rather badly. That is what we observe in the real world.

Redistribution and migration

A cursory exmination would seem to indicate that the percentage of income derived from wealthy people in democracies is an inverse function of the ease with which they can migrate. Very small countries, such as Switzerland, Sweden, and Luxembourg, make no serious effort to collect taxes on the wealthy that are even as large in percentage as they collect from the rest of the population. Medium-sized countries, like Britain,[16] Germany, France, and Italy, are better

---

[14] The inclusion of intellectuals is a subjective guess based on general knowledge. It seems to me likely that the principal beneficiaries of recent changes in the US (and the UK) have been the intellectuals who, through their control of both education and the media, have been able to divert large resources into their own pockets. So far as I know, however, there is no statistical evidence for or against this view.

* Glossary, p. 16.

[15] *Economic Trends*, for the Central Statistical Office, No. 208, HMSO, London, February 1971, Table A, p. x. This probably overstates the transfer from the well-off because of inherent defects in the measurement apparatus (discussed below, p. 23–25).

[16] Recently I visited Athens and my host pointed out the house of a 'typical Greek shipowner'. After I had admired the home, which was about the size of the royal palace but with a better view, my host remarked, 'This is only their summer place; they live in London'. No doubt even Greek shipowners would find it worth paying at least *some* taxes to live in a place as convenient for their business as London, but I

placed to tax the wealthy, and the United States is able to implement substantial *effective* tax progression in top income brackets. In no case, so far as I know, is the progression in the taxes *collected* as steep as in the taxes on paper, but it is nevertheless real in the larger countries.

Benefits reduced by inefficient transfer system

When we turn to expenditures, a different picture emerges. An individual's vote is worth as much as any other individual's vote in getting expenditures. Indeed the wealthy, well-informed person may well be able to obtain a considerably larger portion of the total tax collections than someone without these advantages.[17] If we subtract tax payments from receipts, one would anticipate some 'loss' for the wealthy and perhaps, although not certainly, a 'profit' or breaking even for the rest of the population. The reason why the rest do not necessarily make a 'profit' is the intrinsic inefficiencies in the transfer system. Expenditures will probably cost more than their net benefit.[18] It is therefore possible that, although the rich are injured, the rest of the population make very small 'profits' or even 'losses'.

Thus in democracy we would anticipate some transfer of money away from the wealthy, but there is no obvious reason why it would go to the poor. In the real world, we do find this pattern. It is, however, a relatively minor part of the redistribution of income in the modern state. Economists frequently point out that confiscation of *all* the income of the wealthy in a typical modern state would pay only a tiny part of the routine expenditures of government. Massive movements of money do occur by the political process, but they are not in the main transfers of funds from the wealthy to the poor, *but transfers of funds among the middle class*. The bulk of them come from people between the 20th and the 90th percentile of income, and go to the same income classes. This is, of course, the area with the largest taxable capacity, and also where political power is concentrated in a democracy.

---

doubt if the amount this man would be willing to pay would be very large. Indeed, I feel sure I pay more income taxes in Blacksburg than this vastly wealthy man does in London. No criticism of the British revenue system is implied. Britain is no doubt better off with this shipowner living in London than in Monaco.

[17] Bruno Frey (1971), *op. cit.*

[18] W. A. Niskanen, *Bureaucracy and Representative Government*, Aldine-Atherton, Chicago, 1971.

State education is anti-egalitarian

These transfers do not meet egalitarian criteria. Basically they are transfers from groups of people who for one reason or another are not politically powerful, to people who are; political power, after all, is not evenly distributed within the middle class. Always and everywhere in democracies, the farmers do well. The subsidised government education system is particularly obvious as a redistribution from the mass of non-graduates to the well-off at university. In general, students who can get into a university, particularly those with scholarships, have enough natural talent to enter university with an expected lifetime income well above average. At the expense of the taxpayer, they are then given an even higher lifetime expected income. But even if we turn to lower-level schools, somewhat the same problem exists. To begin with, these are clearly transfers from those in society who do not have children to those who do—to say nothing, of course, of the transfer to the children themselves.

Secondly, however, it is fairly certain that the return to education, even elementary, varies widely, depending on inherited genes and home environment. Thus, the yield in real terms from education is vastly higher to the person who has both the natural talent and the background to have a good income all his life than to the person whose natural talent and background are such that he probably will be poor.

One of the problems with the Nicholson figures (used by Webb and Sieve) on income redistribution is that they take services such as education as a transfer at cost. It certainly is worth much less to the poor than it is to the well-off. Further, it may not be true that the educational system devotes the same resources to each student. Certainly the dull university student with few social graces receives a good deal less attention from his professors than the bright, accomplished student. It seems to me likely that the same situation exists in lower-level educational institutions.* If so, it is likely that in practice students most likely to have a large income during the rest of their lives receive very much more in state-provided resources during their education than do the less well-endowed. The view that state education treats everyone equally has never been subjected to

* [For example, figures recently quoted by Mrs Margaret Thatcher, Britain's Minister of Education, suggest that a high proportion of the best teachers in grammar and comprehensive schools teaches a small number of the brightest pupils in sixth forms (i.e. those expected to go to university).—ED.]

any significant statistical testing. It is possible, although I would not argue certain, that it represents a substantial transfer of resources from the poor to the well-off.

NHS prejudices the poor

The establishment of the National Health Service (NHS) in Britain is a particularly clear example of a welfare measure enacted *against* the interest of the poor. In the 10 years following the enactment of this measure, the death rate among the poorest portion of the British population increased, in spite of the fantastic technological improvements in medicine during this period.[19] This hardly expected development may be explained by a hypothesis. Before the NHS the poor received free (or almost free) medicine on a large scale. The rest of the population, on the other hand, paid for medical attention and hence conserved its use. The NHS made medical treatment free for everyone, and the result was an increase in its consumption by the middle- and upper-classes. Since the total amount of medical resources has not increased—indeed, no new hospitals were built during the first 10 years of the NHS—the increased use of resources by the middle- and upper-classes must have diminished those used for the poor.

Further, the re-arrangement of the way in which doctors were paid gave doctors incentives, albeit not very strong, to shift their practice toward groups with relatively light incidence of disease. This would mean movement away from the poor. The rise in death rate of the poor may therefore not be surprising. Further, the advocates

---

[19] 'For example, the age-specific annual rates of death per 100,000 of population in England and Wales given by the 1951 and 1961 censuses for men within the Registrar General's social classes I and V, as defined in the 1951 census, were these:

	Class I		Class V	
Age Group	1951	1961	1951	1961
25–34	162	76	214	179
35–44	230	165	386	381
45–54	756	528	1,027	1,010
55–64	2,347	1,765	2,567	2,716
65–69	4,839	4,004	4,868	5,142
70–74	7,614	6,278	7,631	8,390

See *The Registrar General's Decennial Supplement for England and Wales, Occupational Mortality, 1951, Part II, Vol. 2*, pp. 23–7; *1961*, unpublished figures from the Registrar General.' (D. Butler and D. Stokes, *Political Change in Britain: Forces Shaping Electoral Choice*, New York, 1969, fn. 1, p. 265.)

of the NHS who may have aimed to aid the poor evidently did not understand what they would be doing, since it clearly did not increase the resources available for them. Must the observer conclude that they intended to benefit the middle-class—which, in the event, they did? It was probably a most inefficient method of transferring resources from the poor to the middle-class. (A good economist could have given advice on better techniques to those who wished to grind the faces of the poor!)[20]

III. INCOME TRANSFERS AND THE MIDDLE CLASSES

These examples are a small part of a wide universe. In most democracies the poor receive relatively minor transfers—in any realistic sense—from society. Very large amounts of money are redistributed by government action but the bulk of it is composed of transfers back and forth within the middle-income brackets. These transfers occur because obtaining such a transfer is a rational investment of resources, and people put their resources into it.

The only astonishing aspect of this phenomenon is that it is so little noted. Almost all the standard discussions of redistribution imply that it is normally from the rich to the poor. Webb and Sieve seem to think that the Welfare State exists to transfer monies to the poor and somehow (by accident?) has been unable to do so. This redistribution is trivial compared to the redistribution within the middle class.* I find the concentration of discussion upon the very *minor* phenomenon of redistribution from the wealthy to the poor and the general ignoring of the *major* phenomenon most remarkable.

Cognitive dissonance

The only explanation I can offer is basically psychological. We must begin with a brief discussion of a well-tested psychological phenomenon: 'reduction of cognitive dissonance'. It is well established that individuals' perception of the world is, to some extent, affected by a subconscious desire to reduce internal tension or 'dissonance'. Thus, an individual will, without dishonesty, believe that activities in accord with motive *A* are also in accord with motive *B*, even if

---

20 Some in Britain apparently believed that the Welfare State would change the conscience of the average Englishman so that he would make sacrifices for the public good or for the poor. If so, it is astonishing that the Welfare State itself does not reflect this 'new consciousness'.

* [In the US the term 'middle-class' is synonymous with 'middle-income group'.—ED.]

objectively they are not. The reason is that he does not wish to admit, even to himself, that he is disregarding motive *B*. Needless to say, this phenomenon occurs only when motive *A* and motive *B* would, in objective terms, lead to different actions and where the individual regards motive *A* as more important than motive *B*.

All of us from childhood have been told it is our duty to be charitable, to help the poor, to do other good acts. But most of us have strong selfish drives. Clearly the injunction that if a man takes your coat, you should give him your cloak also, does not describe what most human beings ordinarily *do*. It is, however, descriptive of what they *say*. Indeed, if I observe my university colleagues, I will find that their expressed *opinions* are largely in accord with the ethically-given drive toward 'loving thy neighbour' and 'giving all you own to the poor'. If I study their *behaviour*, it turns out that they make few sacrifices for the poor.

It is clear they find these two drives—spending your own income yourself and helping the poor—in conflict, and that this should cause some internal tension. I commonly tell my students that if they really want to help the poor they should get two jobs, work as hard as they possibly can, and give all their income to the inhabitants of India, except that minimum amount they need to stay alive. They normally object to this pattern of behaviour, but are normally not willing to admit that the reason they object is simply that they do not *really* feel as charitable as that.[21]

Indeed, if I ask my students, or my faculty colleagues, how much they give to the poor, it usually turns out to be a small amount—in many cases nothing. They commonly explain their attitude by saying they prefer governmental charitable activity. They seldom explain why they should use the government channel for this activity and, in particular, never turn to the perfectly genuine externality arguments for this purpose.[22] They sometimes allege, however, that it is more efficient for them to vote for charity than to make a charitable contribution themselves because state charity brings in other people's money.

Suppose it is suggested I give £100 to the poor, and that either I

[21] In general the farther to the 'left' the individual student, the more incoherent he becomes in dealing with this problem. It is not that the people on the 'right' are willing to admit that they act selfishly, but simply that they are much less embarrassed by the question than the members of the New Left.

[22] For a statement of these reasons by an economist who cannot be accused of socialism, Milton Friedman, *Capitalism and Freedom*, University of Chicago Press, 1962.

take £100 out of my pocket and give it to a charity or we vote on whether I should be taxed £100 to make this charitable payment. The cost to me of making the direct payment is £100. The cost to me of voting for the tax, however, is £100 discounted by my estimate of the influence my vote will have on the outcome. If, say, the constituency is around 100,000, the discounted cost to me of voting for this special tax on myself is vanishingly small. Thus, if I feel a little charitable, I would not make the £100 payment but vote for the tax fully aware that many others are also voting on the same issue and that my vote will make very little difference to the outcome. Thus the cost to me of casting my vote is small. Putting it differently, the public act I am called upon to perform in voting is very low in cost to me, even though it refers to a £100 gift; the private gift is high in cost. Under the circumstances, I would be more likely to vote for forcible charitable activity by everyone than to undertake it myself voluntarily.

Here, also, reduction of cognitive dissonance comes in. If I am possessed both of selfish desires in spending my own money and a feeling that I must be charitable, I should be wise to vote charitably and act selfishly. I should also tend, in discussion, to put much more weight upon the importance of my vote than is justified, and to resent people who tell me that the vote makes almost no difference. At this point, the rationale for the ethical rule that private charity is bad and that all redistribution should be collective becomes apparent. It provides a rationalisation for 'ethical' behaviour in urging government redistribution while making almost no personal sacrifice. It makes possible the best of both worlds.*

The remoter government, the cheaper charity

We can draw further implications. As the size of the constituency increases, the likelihood that a vote will have any effect on the outcome *de*creases. Consider my paying £100 to charity, voting on a tax of £100 to be levied on me by my local government for charitable purposes, voting on a similar tax for similar purposes for a regional or local government, and finally voting on a similar tax for similar purposes by the national government. Clearly, the cost

* [A member of the IEA staff thinks people who advocate collective charity, i.e. requiring others to be charitable, should be asked 'How much should I put you down for?' If charity is giving, is enforced collective giving 'charity'?—ED.]

to me is monotonically* decreasing through this set. I would be more likely to vote for the tax by the national government than for the regional government, for the tax by the regional government than for the local government, and more likely to vote for the tax by the local government than to make the direct payment myself. This phenomenon may explain the tendency to transfer charitable activity from local governments to the national government. Looked at from the standpoint of the voter, he can obtain the satisfaction of 'behaving charitably' in a national election much more cheaply than he can in the local election.[23]

Is over-investment in charity likely?

The reasoning so far would indicate that voting on charitable issues might lead to vast over-investment in charity. I doubt whether this is so. First, the pattern of drives that leads to reduction in the internal cognitive dissonance I have been describing is limited largely to the upper classes. We intellectuals are the primary holders of these attitudes and we make up only a minority of the population. The majority are much less prone to this type of thinking, and hence we are free to cast votes in this way without it costing us very much.

There is, however, another phenomenon that might conceivably put us in the 'prisoner's dilemma'.* Intellectuals may not vote for charity, but they certainly *talk* about it a good deal! (p. 27). In the average university community the individual who said flatly that he was opposed to charity because he liked to spend his money himself would be subject to very large private 'costs' of unpopularity, rejection or persecution. But favouring charitable activities and engaging in political activity in their behalf will normally have a distinct private return. Thus the average intellectual who might or

* Glossary, p. 16.

[23] There is the possibility of a 'prisoner's dilemma' here which might lead to the voting decision being the one which is binding. Suppose a proposal is made to tax everyone in Britain, with more than £2,000 a year income, £50 to distribute to the poor. Each person might feel his vote carried practically no weight and he could gain some pleasure from voting for charitable activity, and hence vote for it. This would mean that the act would pass and everyone would be charged £50. There is no miscalculation here. As in the usual prisoner's dilemma, the individual would be correct in his assessment of the cost to him of voting for or against this tax. The aggregation of the votes would mean, however, that he found himself in the lower right-instead of the upper left-hand corner of the prisoner's dilemma matrix, and would put out more money for charity than he really wants. He is attempting to buy at a discount the feeling of satisfaction which comes from a 'charitable act', and finds he has to pay the full price.

might not be inclined to vote in the way we have described generally finds it pays to engage in political activity in favour of government charity.

It is possible that over long periods of time this might change the general opinion of society so that the government would become more charitable, and hence the 'prisoner's dilemma' might exist in the long run by way of the opinion-forming process. I think it does not; my reasons require a little more elaboration on the structure of democratic electoral systems.

So far the reasoning has assumed that there are direct votes on charitable transfers. We do not observe this in the real world. The situation in the USA or UK democracy is that we vote only periodically, and that our vote conveys relatively little information (in the technical sense) to the politician. Parties offer a whole collection of issues and proposals to the electorate, and are elected or not in terms of the whole package. The weight of their view on any given issue in determining the election is hard to determine. In general it is fairly clear that most politicians regard transfer of funds by government process as *mainly* a way of purchasing the votes of the people who *receive* them, not of those who *give* them.

Would the poor do better on charity than with votes?

Thus a party seeking the vote of university professors will normally make a song and dance about how we must help the poor. This is, however, merely an effort to reduce the 'cognitive dissonance' in the professors' minds. What counts is emphasis on how important the party thinks it is that academic research be stimulated, that education receive larger funds, that the income-tax law be provided with loopholes for academics, etc. The academic is normally quite capable of rationalising all these bounties into a charitable activity, particularly if the party also makes some remarks about helping the poor. The end-product is not that the 'prisoner's dilemma' leads to an over-investment in charity, but that the pressure groups—including the pressure group of the intellectuals—get very large transfers.

This phenomenon has led me to speculate whether the poor might not do better if they depended on pure charity rather than on an attempt to use the weight of their votes to acquire tax funds. It seems to me at least conceivable that if *all* people who receive a significant part of their funds from any government office were deprived of a vote in electing the government, the poor would do better than they do now.

IV. POLICY OPTIONS

So far this essay as been descriptive and has avoided advocacy. The bulk of my readers will feel it is essentially a destruction of wrong thinking. They probably expect me now to provide a remedy. I am not at all sure the situation requires a remedy. Individuals who are deriving a feeling of being charitable without much real cost through their use of the political process are maximising their individual preferences, and would be injured, i.e. have a lower level of satisfaction, if they were compelled to make a more objectively accurate calculation of the real effects of their behaviour. Should democratic government not provide this type of satisfaction to the voters?

Three solutions

For those, however, who are uneasy and wish to 'do something', I can suggest three possible courses of action. The first—and the one I am sure most people who are disturbed by the essay will take—is simply to deny that it is true and continue happily reducing cognitive dissonance by combining selfishness in private expenditures and 'generosity' in politics. For most, I think, this course of action will maximise their satisfaction: course *A*.

For those who find it impossible, there are two remaining options. They can take action to bring reality into accord with what is said, i.e. they can try to make people be as charitable in their actions as they are in their language: course B. Conversely, they can try to make people talk as they act, i.e. change people's statements so that they accurately describe what they *do*, rather than being mere professions of loyalty to the prevailing ideals: course C.

I would prefer course C* and, indeed, I suspect that, if we could somehow carry it out, the poor would get rather more money than they do now. Granted that transfer to the poor is now muddled up with truly massive transfers to other people, the voter quite rationally tries to restrict the total volume of the transfer. I think if permitted

* [My colleague would like course B, in which people advocating collective charity enforced by taxation would 'put down' an amount to represent their private giving with personal sacrifice. It would be intriguing to decide the size of the amount 'put down'. Should it be a full sum irrespective of means? a proportion of means? Should it be progressive? regressive? Should it be the requirement for a vote on redistributive taxation?—ED.]

to vote on direct payments to the poor, he would probably choose to give them more. This, of course, is a guess.[24]

Thus, if it is thought desirable to 'do something', it is easier to change the way we *talk* than the way we *behave*. Further, if we do change the way we talk, we will be better informed about the real world (including the preferences of ourselves and our friends), and hence are likely to behave more effectively. Not least, the poor, along with the rest of us, would benefit from the change.

24 When people have been asked to make a choice between universal and selective methods of welfare provision, they have almost invariably chosen selective transfers. British surveys of public preferences in social welfare are discussed in two IEA Research Monographs by Arthur Seldon: No. 8, *Universal or Selective Social Benefits?*, February 1967, and No. 14, *Taxation and Welfare*, November 1967.

3. *Quids* without *Quos*—A Praxeological Approach*

A. J. CULYER

Assistant Director, Institute of Social and Economic Research, University of York

'For a long time men failed to realise that the transition from the classical theory of value to the subjective theory of value was much more than the substitution of a more satisfactory theory of market exchange for a less satisfactory one. The general theory of choice and preference goes far beyond the horizon which encompassed the scope of economic problems as circumscribed by the economists from Cantillon, Hume, and Adam Smith down to John Stuart Mill. It is much more than merely a theory of the "economic side" of human endeavours and of man's striving for commodities and an improvement in his material well-being. *It is the science of every kind of human action.*

Choosing determines all human decisions. In making his choice man chooses not only between various *material* things and services. *All* human values are offered for option. All ends and means, both material and ideal issues, the sublime and the base, the noble and the ignoble, are ranged in a single row and subjected to a decision which picks out one thing and sets aside another. Nothing that men aim at or want to avoid remains outside of this arrangement into a unique scale of graduation and preference. The modern theory of value widens the scientific horizon and enlarges the field of economic studies. Out of the political economy of the classical school emerges the general theory of human action, *praxeology*.'

LUDWIG VON MISES
Human Action (1949)

---

* I have been much aided by the penetrating comments received on an early draft of this paper from Messrs Ron Akehurst, Bengt Jönsson and Alan Maynard, and Professors Armen Alchian, Alan Peacock, Gordon Tullock and Jack Wiseman. In view of the wide ramifications discussed or implied in this essay the usual exonerations from responsibility are more than usually appropriate.

THE AUTHOR

A. J. CULYER was born in 1942 and is married with two children. He is Assistant Director of the Institute of Social and Economic Research and a Senior Lecturer in the Department of Economics and Related Studies at the University of York. His publications include numerous papers in professional journals on economic theory, welfare economics and economic and social policy, and he is the author of *Economics of Social Policy* (Martin Robertson, London, 1973). He is the research director of a programme of economic studies in health care at York, and, in addition to his own work in this programme and other areas, is jointly engaged with Professor Jack Wiseman in an SSRC-financed research project in the economics of charities.

I. HOW TO STICK TO ONE'S LAST WITHOUT APPEARING TO

In this essay the charge may be warranted that I am not sticking to my last, for I intend, in an exploratory way, to tread precisely where most professionals (even the more angelic of them) usually durst not, by investigating the highly controversial area of gift 'transactions'. Von Mises's apothegm nailed to the masthead of this essay implies that the economic (or, as he terms it, the praxeological) approach need not be interpreted in a narrow sense. Indeed, one of the purposes is to push the approach as far as possible, thus invading what will appear thoroughly *non-economic* territory, to see what insights can be gained.

This essay is no more than a starting point for the analysis of giving. It explores key concepts which serve to show, if nothing else, that unique interpretations of the gift phenomenon should be treated with caution. It may thus assist in identifying testable theories to discover which, if any, is the more or most plausible. The framework suggested for thinking about 'gifts' appears to meld moderately well with many of the basic facts associated with giving. The framework also suggests many ethical issues I had not anticipated.

II. THE ECONOMICS OF GIVING?

'The idea that everything has its price may expose us to the charge of cynicism but it should at least save us from the charge of a false absolutism.'

KENNETH BOULDING
Notes on a Theory of Philanthropy (1962)

A useful starting point is to be found in an historical controversy in anthropological literature concerning the form and functions of giving, which touches or focusses on its economic aspects. The act of giving, whether by individuals or communities, has been well documented since the earliest times by students of primitive societies. At first it appears to have been interpreted by outside observers, observing the reciprocal nature of some gift relationships, as a form of primitive and highly ritualised barter. Since barter and exchange form an easily recognisable part of the subject matter of economics it was natural to place an 'economic', 'utilitarian', interpretation upon them. The characteristics of this interpretation were (to simplify but not over-simplify) two-fold: that the motive behind giving gifts was *selfish*, and that the gifts themselves were physical objects of practical usefulness.

It soon became clear that this crude utilitarianism gave an inadequate account of the function of giving in primitive societies. For example, Tom Harrison wrote of the New Hebrideans, amongst whom he lived:

'If a man shoots a hawk—which is very difficult, for they seldom come to earth except to rest in far places—that hawk belongs by right to his chief. When the chief has paid the shooter a pig, and has himself taken the best feathers for his sacred ornaments, the whole village will take this lovely bird and one very valuable pig, a twice-circled-tusker, to another village. They will present this pig and the bird (with the usual numerous formalities) to the chief of that village. And that village will take the bird and cook it in the bush far from the women (it is so holy); there every man eats a fragment of this highest killer. Then they must strive to repay the gift; until they have done so they may not go to war against the donors'.[1]

Concerning individual gifts:

'When a Hebridean is given a present, he shows no gratitude. The explanation is simple; he shows none because he feels none. In this society, where every man can have more than enough by his own effort, the exchange of presents has been raised into a system of rivalry, a process of over-production by the more vigorous who give to others, who must then strive to return the gift. By this means no man is content with enough; everyone lives on his toes, competing in giving'.[2]

Ritualised giving

The complex function of giving revealed in these quotations is sufficient to refute the crude utilitarian approach to giving which Malinowski (of whom more anon) had also been at pains to destroy.[3] Instead, what we observe is a highly ritualised form of giving, often with religious overtones, by which inter-tribal relations are, in part, regulated and hierarchies within and between communities established and maintained. An interesting aspect of Harrison's account is that he asserts an abundance of physical economic goods (and hence an absence of any economic problem in their production and distribution) but a chronic scarcity of other (economic) goods such as prestige and power. The implications are not without interest to social philosophers of the idealist school who anticipate an end to material scarcity and the abolition of the economic problem: the

1 Tom Harrison, *Savage Civilisation*, Gollancz, London, 1937, pp. 34–35.

2 *Ibid.*, p. 343.

3 Bronislaw Malinowski, *Argonauts of the Western Pacific*, Routledge, London, 1922, p. 166 ff.

'economy of abundance' may prove to have more intractable social problems than the economies in which we currently, perforce, live.

The 'potlatch' of the North-West American Chinooks (an aggressive form of obligatory giving by one tribe to another) appears to have been a common feature of all primitive societies. It seems that from the earliest times man has sought to maintain ascendancy over others by regulating their indebtedness to him. (Doubtless such motives also underly much of the giving observed in contemporary western society.) The 'potlatch' of the Indians; the 'kula' of the Trobriand Islanders (a highly sophisticated 'potlatch' among the aristocrats of various tribes in which special articles circulate for ever in a kind of perpetual inter-tribal trade, of great magical and social significance for givers and receivers, binding tribes together); the 'Kerekere' season in Fiji, when all that a man asks you must give; all these and many similar gift-relationships in primitive societies have little to do with what Malinowski called 'economic' man:

> 'the conception of a rational being who wants nothing but to satisfy his simplest needs and does it according to the economic principle of least effort. The economic man always knows exactly where his material interests lie, and makes for them in a straight line.'[4]

Even the sacrificial destruction of wealth in primitive North-West American and North-East Asian 'potlatch' implies giving something. According to Marcel Mauss,

> 'it is not simply to show power and wealth and unselfishness that a man puts his slaves to death, burns his precious oil, throws copper into the sea, and sets his house on fire. In doing this he is also sacrificing to the gods and spirits.'[5]

The economic model of man properly developed and interpreted (the prime concern of this essay) is not inconsistent with such events and we shall use it to investigate a far broader range of phenomena. Thus, although we shall retain an interest in primitive economies—and in their students—we shall eschew primitive economics.

Tangibility and physical dimensions are thus not necessary conditions for the application of economics. What of an apparently far more intractable problem: the absence of reciprocity; pure altruism; '*genuine*' giving by one brought up in a culture historically condi-

---

[4] *Ibid.*, p. 516.

[5] Marcel Mauss, *The Gift*, Cohen and West, London, 1966, p. 14.

tioned by the traditional Christian teaching on ideal behaviour or Aristotle's notion of the liberal or munificent man? The genuine gift, in what von Mises termed 'autistic exchange', is a *quid* with no *quo*, not self-advancement nor even self-satisfaction nor glows of charitable warmth. As Professor Kenneth Boulding has put it:

> 'it is this capacity, for empathy—for putting oneself in another's place, for feeling the joys and sorrows of another as one's own—which is the source of the genuine gift . . . this is "charity" before the word became corrupted by vanity and fashion.'[6]

If it can be shown that altruism of this sort is as readily incorporated into economics as selfishness, one would be well on the road to re-establishing political economy as a general theory of society, paving the way for the ultimate reconciliation of our over-compartmentalised social science(s). In the nature of the task we are opening up wide-ranging vistas of which we can at present indicate only some principal landmarks and outlines.

Selfishness and altruism

> A man there was, tho some did count him mad,
> The more he cast away, the more he had.
>
> JOHN BUNYAN
> *The Pilgrim's Progress*

Even at the definitional stage the economic approach has some insights to offer. Some of the key inferences will be based upon the distinctions drawn here. One such distinction is between 'selfishness' and 'altruism'.

A selfish person is one for whom the well-being of others is of no concern. An altruistic person is one for whom it is of concern. The sources of well-being are many and varied. They may be worthy or unworthy objects of desire; sacred or profane; divisible or indivisible; traded or untraded; necessarily shared with others (peace) or private (bread). The selfish person is indifferent to the quantities had by other people: he wants more of them for his own use. The altruist *in addition* to wanting more for himself, also wants more for others. If one relevant entity is 'housing', the altruist would like more for himself and for others. In a sense he is 'better off'

[6] Kenneth E. Boulding, 'Notes on a Theory of Philanthropy', in Frank G. Dickinson (ed.), *Philanthropy and Public Policy*, NBER, Columbia University Press, London, 1962, p. 61.

when others have more. We could if we wished (at the risk of inviting the derision of economist-baiters) say that the altruist derives 'utility' from the consumption (in a very broad sense) of others as well as from his own.[7] The choice problem for the altruist may apply not only to dividing resources between his own use and someone else's but also—even if he does not value some of them *at all* in his own use—among the (competing) uses of others. Even saints have to economise.

Consider the choice problem of the perfectly altruistic man. In practice he will *not* be readily identifiable although he gives all his wealth, time and all else he has to others. The pattern of preferences corresponding to the man who gives away his all may be of two kinds. His preferences may be described as above but his concern for others may be so strong, and the subjective costs of foregoing self-gratification so low, that he never in practice chooses any entity for his own use. Alternatively, selfish desires may simply not figure among his preferences at all. This distinction may correspond to a theological distinction: the presence of objects of desire for own use implying the existence of 'original sin', or 'temptation'. Their absence implies the absence of temptation to sin if we take selfish motives as sinful. Thus, preferences that include selfish and altruistic elements, coupled with behaviour such that no selfish one is chosen in practice, may depict a St Francis, or Christ-made-Man. Possession of a set of preferences in which entities for one's own use are totally absent may depict Man before the Fall (though it is not altogether clear whether Adam and Eve faced the economic problem as starkly as we have since then. Nevertheless, we know about them precisely because they faced a problem of choice). Dostoevsky's Grand Inquisitor played merry by fudging the distinction drawn here in his condemnation of Christ for giving Free Will to mankind. One of his arguments was that only the strong could be saved and that the weak are inevitably damned. His solution was to raise the cost of acquiring (some of) the entities for one's own use to infinity, thereby forcing men to (appear to) be good—a truly satanical solution in the

[7] The selfish person's utility function may be written:
$U^A = U^A (x_1{}^A, x_2{}^A, x_3{}^A, \ldots, x_n{}^A)$,where A indicates an individual.
The altruist's is:
$U^A = U^A (x_1{}^A, x_2{}^A, \ldots, x_n{}^A; x_1{}^B, \ldots, x_n{}^B; x_1{}^C, \ldots, x_n{}^C; \ldots, x_n{}^N)$, and
$\partial U^A | \partial x_i^B > 0$ if $\partial U^B | \partial x_i^B > 0$, where B, C, ... N are other persons.
The perfect altruist has $U^A = U^A (x_i^B, \ldots, x_n^B; x_i^C \ldots, x_n^C; \ldots; x_n^N)$.

best intellectual tradition attributed to the master of darkness. Morality was achieved by *force majeure*.

Egalitarianism

How does the well-being of others enter into an individual's preferences? For an egalitarian, what may matter is not the absolute but the relative quantities of the entities. There are some interesting possibilities. One is that an individual is concerned with the absolute quantity of entities for his own use but that, in his concern for the rest of society, it is the differences from the average level that matters.[8]

Clearly, mere concern with equality *for others* as here can imply both levelling up *and* levelling down. The equality objective can then be attained entirely by levelling down, the surplus entities going to the altruist. The basic preferences of egalitarians who advocate more equality yet play the stock exchange for what it is worth on the ground that, until the egalitarian millenium is reached, an unjust system should be milked for what one can get, is rather like this. It also seems to describe Professor Sir Alfred Ayer's preferences quite well:

'If the independent schools enjoy an educational advantage, it is mainly because the more privileged parents continue to send their children to them. So, if one believes in social equality, should not one set an example by having one's children educated in the public sector, even at some small cost to them? This would be a very strong argument, if there were any great likelihood that one's example would be widely followed; but in fact there is not . . . Political action will be needed to strip them of their privileged positions . . . In the meantime, like most parents, we shall do what appears to be the most advantageous for our son'.[9]

Alternatively, an individual may choose to reduce his *own* use of an entity if it is above average and to increase it if it is below as well as reducing discrepancies between averages and other people's ownership. This again implies both levelling up and levelling down.[10] It also has its dangers. As Bernard Shaw somewhere shrewdly remarked, self-sacrifice enables us unblushingly to sacrifice others.

---

[8] For example:
$U^A = U^A\,(x_1{}^A, x_2{}^A, \ldots, x_n{}^A; |\bar{x}_1 - x_1{}^B|, \ldots, |\bar{x}_n - x_n{}^B|; \ldots, |\bar{x}_n - x_n{}^N|).$

[9] *Sunday Times*, 16 July, 1967.

[10] The implied utility function is:
$U^A = U^A\,(|\bar{x}_1 - x_1{}^A|, |\bar{x}_2 - x_2{}^A|, \ldots, |\bar{x}_n - x_n{}^A|; |\bar{x}_1 - x_1{}^B|, \ldots, |\bar{x}_n - x_n{}^B|; \ldots, |\bar{x}_n - x_n{}^N|).$

III. SOME POLITICS OF GIVE AND TAKE

'Benevolent people are very apt to be one-sided and fussy, and not of the sweetest temper if others will not be good and happy in their way.'

Sir Arthur Helps
Friends in Council (1873)

A philosophical difficulty with egalitarian altruism is that, although levelling up and levelling down need not necessarily harm anybody, we have no means of telling unless the levelling down is performed by the altruist *on himself*. As soon as he begins levelling down operations on others, as well as himself, it becomes impossible to say whether this is consistent with *their* preferred choices. Nor would it be possible to say for society *as a whole*, as compared with the altruist alone, whether there had been any net improvement in the distribution of resources. A similar difficulty applies to other, non-egalitarian, types of altruism, for the altruist may benefit also if someone else gives something away rather than himself. In short, the inter-dependencies between the preferences discussed can provide the 'praxeological' basis, or economic explanation, for the coercive elements in human relationships.

Coercion and freedom

A preference for or against coercion will arise only when such inter-dependencies exist; but it suggests, in turn, another kind of inter-dependence between individuals' preferences. Whether or not an individual seeks to implement his preferred choices with coercion (rather than, say, compensation) is itself a choice problem and should properly therefore be incorporated into the praxeological approach. A 'liberal', who characteristically opposes choices being imposed upon others, is attaching a relatively high weight to 'freedom from imposed choice' which would constitute one of the elements in his (expanded) set of preferences. By the same token, he places a low weight (possibly zero) upon 'others' freedom from having to make choices'. He accordingly opposes coerced choice but will not object to coercing other individuals *to choose*. The so-called paradox of liberalism, that men are forced to be free, is not really a paradox, but merely a statement about the preferences characteristically held by liberals. Conversely, an 'authoritarian' would characteristically reverse this ranking, placing a relatively low weight upon 'freedom from imposed choice' (not necessarily a zero weight, however) and a high weight on 'others' freedom from having to make choices'. Given equal disapproval of the things others do, the liberal is less likely to force them to do otherwise by imposing his own preferences.[11]

Altruism and generosity

> 'Are things what they seem?
> Or is visions about?'
>
> KEATS
> *Ode to a Nightingale*

Of the variety of motives that may inspire giving, some admirable, other less admirable, we shall consider only the 'ultimate' one of pure altruism—the desire to help others. Not least among the reasons for selecting this highest and most admirable of motives is that it is popularly regarded as least economic. Clearly, on some definitions of economics (for example, as the study of commercial relationships) giving must be counted as non-economic. If, alternatively, by economic is meant implying choice, giving is an economic matter (as well, of course, as being sociological, anthropological political, ethical, . . .).

The definition of altruism says nothing about *generosity*. Indeed, our approach enables us to make a very clear distinction between altruism and generosity. If an altruistic person is one for whom the well-being of others is of concern, i.e. *he cares*, all this information conveys is that the well-being of others has a *positive weight* in his set of preferences. It does not tell us whether, under any given circumstance, he will perform good works. In short, altruism is not a *behavioural* concept. Whether or not an altruistic person presents others with gifts depends upon the circumstances, for example the

[11] Economists' customary use of the Pareto criterion seems to assume implicitly that individuals derive utility from neither kind of freedom—freedom to choose and freedom from having to choose. Thus, though they have been much mixed up, liberal and Paretian economics (as customarily discussed) are not the same thing at all. If the Paretian approach were expanded to incorporate these—and, indeed, other—elements into individual preferences, liberal and Paretian economics could diverge more than they usually do. For example, the provision of a wider range of goods from which to choose would normally be counted a 'good thing' on both liberal and Paretian criteria (the latter provided that the extended range included some goods that were actually chosen). If some individuals were, however, averse to choice *per se* (as some surely are) the expanded Paretian approach would not be able to determine whether this were good or bad. Indeed, if some individuals were averse to choice and others were indifferent and no compensation were offered, it would be accounted unambiguously *bad*—the opposite of the liberal conclusion!

intensity of the desire of one individual to give to another *and* the costs of giving. An altruistic person may feel compassion for a family with no home but he is *not* bound by our definition of 'altruism' to surrender his own home. Thus, *generosity* is a function of the environment in which a person lives as well as the degree to which he is altruistic (glad they are not poor); an altruist may not feel the necessity of generous acts. If his fellow beings are not well off, even though he is altruistic (desires to help them), he may not do so if the costs are sufficiently high.

Furthermore (supposing him to be generous as well as altruistic), he may not give individually to another. He may *combine* with others to give to an individual or a group. Such *collective* gifts may be organised privately (e.g. charities) or in the government sector (the 'welfare state').

Implications of the distinction between altruism and generosity

The distinction between altruism and generosity has important consequences. One is that it is not possible to infer from *behaviour* the extent to which individuals are altruistic. An altruistic person may not give anything because the circumstances are not appropriate (e.g. the personal costs are too high). A selfish person who appears to give freely may be doing so under external duress or in anticipation of personal gain. Although (for discussion) we have ruled out the latter possibility by concentrating on genuinely altruistic individuals, many gifts are, in practice, made with personal gain in mind. A substantial function of the gift-relationships in primitive societies was to further the status of individuals and groups. One test for whether the motive for giving is the expectation of reciprocal gifts is that, if reciprocal gifts tend not to be forthcoming, the originating source of gifts will dry up. Anger may be expressed.[12] Other motives may be moral blackmail, or the desire to establish relationships which place the recipient under an obligation to the donor. Thus, true motivation is, in practice, exceedingly difficult to establish.

Another implication is that an unambiguous indicator of a person's degree of altruism is not given by the quantity or frequency of the market exchange value of his gifts. The widow's mite may (or may not) be a more *altruistic* act than the abundance of a (generous) Dives. Unfortunately again we have no method of measuring the

---

[12] In primitive society, the ideal was to give a 'potlatch' that could not be returned, for the person who could not reciprocate lost rank and possibly even his status as a free man.

subjective value to an individual of what he gives away, which is the true indicator of his altruism: a deficiency recognised by theologians long before social scientists espoused the 'scientific impossibility of inter-personal utility comparisons'. In most of the great religions in which free will is acknowledged, the assessment is left not to man but to God. Man is specifically invoked *not* to judge his fellows by their actions.

A third important implication is that voluntarily given gifts may not be given *freely*. One may let part of one's house to the homeless family at a reduced but nevertheless positive price. This implication follows from the assertion that generosity (as distinct from altruism) depends also on the terms upon which altruism may be expressed. By giving away something at a reduced price an individual can implement altruistic motives which he may choose not to implement if he were constrained to give at a zero price.

Failure to notice that generosity is a function of the terms under which gifts are given can lead to tendentious dispute. In the recent controversy over payment for blood donors, for example, the distinction implies that a broad division between donors and 'professional' suppliers of blood is neither morally (if only motives count) nor practically useful. On the moral side the distinction implies either that one is God or that one is making explicit (but fruitless) inter-personal utility comparisons, for the more altruistic person confronted by different constraints may give less than the less altruistic person. The distinction is meaningless, for it hides the implication that genuinely altruistic blood donors would donate even more than they do if the terms of donation were made more favourable,[13] or that, for equally altruistic persons, the one for whom the costs of transferring resources from own-use to others'-use are lower will be more generous.

The distinction between altruism and generosity is not merely pedantic. It is crucial for social policy. The reason is that we do not currently understand the mechanisms that determine the relative weights of elements in individuals' sets of preferences. We do not, in other words, have any generally accepted theory of what makes people more or less

---

[13] M. H. Cooper and A. J. Culyer, *The Price of Blood*, Hobart Paper 41, IEA, London, 1968; R. M. Titmuss, *The Gift Relationship*, Allen and Unwin, London, 1970; M. H. Cooper and A. J. Culyer, 'The Economics of Giving and Selling Blood', below, Part II, Essay 1, p. 109.

altruistic.[14] There is, of course, evidence that childhood upbringing can affect these weights in fairly predictable ways, but we have no theory that indicates the role social policy, as such, can play. By contrast, we have a theory, or the beginnings of one, about generosity. We *can* specify some of the influences that will make a person more or less generous. Compensation is one. The use of collective organisations is another (below, p. 52). These influences reintroduce *quos* to correspond to specific *quids*. But the *quos* need not appeal to the *selfish* motives of individuals (p. 53). The distinction between altruism and generosity opens up the possibility of a wide variety of different types of *quo*, some of which may be altogether different from the *quos* of market exchange (a form of reciprocal, but contractual, giving). Generosity, as compared with altruism, is subject to the law of demand.

IV. MORALS AND POLICY IN BLOOD SUPPLY

'If we desire to hand on to the afterworld our direct influence, and not merely the memory of our excellence, we must take even more care to improve the social organism of which we form part, than to perfect our own individual developments.'

SIDNEY WEBB
Fabian Essays (1908)

In his *The Gift Relationship*, ostensibly dealing with a 'social philosophy' of giving, Titmuss[15] did not unfortunately delve into these problems. His entire analysis was related to only one species of gift, namely blood donation (itself a rather special case discussed in more detail in the second half of this book), and his purpose throughout was more to defend the holistic principle of blood donation by the means available to him than to analyse it in a thorough examination of the gift-relationship itself. Unfortunately, it is not easy to extract the core of his analysis, but one thing is certainly clear from it; he placed heavy emphasis on the ethical importance of altruism (as here defined) as well as upon generosity (though he did not distinguish the two). Although he evaluated gift-relationships in human blood supply sometimes in terms of an economic 'cost-benefit' framework (the validity of which he was sceptical about), a major

[14] If all the other factors affecting generosity could be held constant, an increase in generous behaviour would imply an increase in altruism. It would still, however, be impossible to tell who was more altruistic than others. All one could assert was that some individuals were more altruistic than they had been previously.

[15] *Op. cit.*

argument he deployed was the profound importance of the spirit of altruism in society—the necessity of a re-affirmation that man is a moral being.

The erosion of moral standards and of charity is a disquieting phenomenon—and a recurring one in human history. It is not the purpose to question this view here. What *is* questionable is the extent to which the *motives* of men, as distinct from their *actions*, are shaped or can be affected by social policy. I frankly do not see any practical possibilities by which a new generation of altruistic individuals with one-tenth of the qualities of the greatest saints of Christendom can be brought up by the application of principles derived from any of the social sciences, let alone converting present generations having *tabula* that are far from *rasa*. But there is abundant evidence that, given their motives, *behaviour* can be manipulated. In short, the private costs and the private rewards that individuals pay or receive must be so adjusted that their *behaviour* corresponds to the socially desirable. This is how the 'social organism' can be improved and it is the customary basis from which social science begins.

If existing generosity, given its constraints, is not sufficient to produce the quantity of whole blood the Americans feel they need, or to alleviate the poverty we abhor, or to provide the education our youngsters require, the constraints should be changed. This will not remove all argument about policy because the constraints can be altered in various ways. Even if we could all agree about what was required, we may not agree on the effectiveness or on the consequences of various means of getting it. But at least the policy debate would have been raised (or lowered) to a level at which social scientists can reasonably be regarded as competent.

V. MEANS AND ENDS

'In the welter of conflicting fanaticisms, one of the few unifying forces is scientific truthfulness, by which I mean the habit of basing our beliefs upon observations and inferences as impersonal, and as much divested of local and temperamental bias, as is possible for human beings.'

BERTRAND RUSSELL
History of Western Philosophy (1946)

What appears to be the prevailing approach to gift-relationships? To the economic mind it appears to be one-sided and arbitrary, and not surprisingly has led some into one-sided and arbitrary conclusions. It is founded upon a *functionalist* approach in the analysis of giving and gift-relationships.

The functionalist approach

According to the functionalist approach in the anthropological (and much sociological) literature, social institutions, such as giving, are interpreted as contributing towards an ultimate objective of a society or culture. Frequently, such objectives are drawn very broadly and consist in such aims as the *survival* of the culture, or social cohesion. Rain-making ceremonials in primitive cultures may be recognised as not very functional in making rain but as 'functional' in providing a periodic corporate identity to the tribe or group. The functionalist approach seeks to *explain* social institutions by reference to hypothesised social objectives. Some extreme functionalists, such as Malinowski, even appear to have taken the view that *all* social institutions are functional and that each is, moreover, essential:

> 'The functional view of culture *insists* therefore upon the principle that in every type of civilisation, every custom, material object, idea and belief fulfils some vital function, has some task to accomplish, represents some indispensable part within a working whole.'[16]

While this 'naïve functionalism' may be criticised on the ground that it begs the very question that ought to be asked, its virtue is that it attempts to explain all phenomena in terms of a general and consistent theoretical framework.

Naïve functionalism is, nevertheless, a menace, for it lends a spurious intellectualism to extremist ideology. Indeed, it is sometimes hard to distinguish it from ideology itself. The dangers are basically two-fold. One is that it tends to be associated with the view that an observed cultural institution is also *necessary* (possibly even *sufficient*) for fulfilling a function. The second is that the *end* is often thought unique.

Functionalism and ethics

Both dangers were present in Titmuss's discussion of the gift-relationship. If giving freely to unnamed recipients is eroded by commercialism and men say

> ' "I need no longer experience (or suffer from) a sense of responsibility (or sin) in not giving to my neighbour" then the consequences are likely to be socially

[16] Bronislaw Malinowski, 'Anthropology', *Encyclopaedia Britannica*, First Supplementary Volume, London, 1926, p. 132.

pervasive. There is nothing permanent about the expression of reciprocity. If the bonds of community giving are broken the result is not a state of value neutralism. The vacuum is likely to be filled by hostility and social conflict . . .'[17]

Rarely can such a prophesy of doom have been derived from so modest a sociological theory. Even more remarkable is this Boanerges's invitation to believe that such are the consequences of paying *blood donors*! These eccentric conclusions are, however, inherent in naïve functionalism—the belief that an institution uniquely fulfils a function.

Titmuss's assiduous work in this subject tended also to succumb to the second danger inherent in naïve functionalism, by ignoring (or assuming away) the possibility of conflicting social goals:

'In a positive sense we believe that policy and processes should enable men to be free to choose to give [blood] to unnamed strangers.'[18]

The freedom here referred to consists in the freedom to give or not to give. It *excludes* the freedom to sell blood and to choose the recipient because:

'private market systems . . . not only deprive men of their freedom to choose to give or not to give but by so doing escalate other coercive forces in the social system which lead to the denial of other freedoms . . .'[19]

Titmuss's view of freedom tended to be coercive (as defined, p. 41). Like the Grand Inquisitor, who underrated the importance of faith (and crucified Christ a second time), he tended to underrate the importance of *altruism* in ethics. Moreover this approach underrated the importance of *generosity* in policy.

Nevertheless, if we follow the spirit of his discussion by supposing that such freedom, in his sense, is an objective, and accept that only voluntary blood donation serves this end,[20] we may define this function of blood donation as *latent* contrasted with the *overt* function: getting enough high-quality blood to meet clinical requirements. The overt function is that for which the institution was consciously

---

[17] Titmuss, *op. cit.*, p. 199.

[18] Titmuss, *op. cit.*, p. 242. He continued: 'They should not be coerced or constrained by the market. In the interests of the freedom of all men they should not, however, be free to sell their blood or decide on the specific destination of the gift.' The freedom offered by Titmuss is thus similar to that offered by the Grand Inquisitor—the freedom to do good, and good alone—in correcting the work of Christ. But Titmuss granted also the freedom to do nothing.

[19] Titmuss, *op. cit.*, p. 239.

[20] But again only for the sake of argument. Actually, we reject both assertions.

designed; the latent is unintended, indirect and was possibly even unperceived. Titmuss, of course, brought the latent function to the centre of the stage and believed anyway that the overt function was most effectively fulfilled by donation alone (because of the hepatitis risk in bought blood). He consequently overlooked the ethical connotations of the overt function by concentrating on those of the latent function, just as he overlooked the effectiveness of the latent function by concentrating on that of the overt function. Gift-relationships in general, he argued, as well as in the specific case of blood distribution, signify 'fellowship' with society in general, a good and moral objective that can be encouraged by social policy. Who could possibly disagree? It is indeed a latent and desirable function of blood donation to promote 'fellowship'. But because donation, like many other acts of giving, has more than one ethical function it also serves more than one ethical end, for saving lives—others' lives—(the overt function) must surely be regarded as no less ethically based and socially desirable than 'fellowship'. Indeed, it is an overt and concrete example of an invisible and generalised 'fellowship'. But it is not the same as the latent function, for saving the lives of others can also be accomplished by *selling* blood (and other things) as well as *giving*, while 'fellowship' in the Titmuss sense cannot.

Here lies the ethical conflict, for no sooner is it postulated that blood selling may save more lives than blood giving, than the *means to an ethical end* conflicts with the means *that is an end in itself*. This ethical conflict, which is real and important, is denied by the Titmuss confusion of latent and overt functions and by the emphasis on a single ethical end. The conflict, moreover, is not denied by the current higher risk of death from bought blood than from donated blood, for more of an imperfect thing may be preferable to less of a perfect thing, especially if there is a chronic shortage.*

If the overt function is the production of sufficient quantities of human blood to meet clinical requirements, blood selling is 'functional' since it produces some blood for clinical use. But it is 'dysfunctional' in that it also, given current methods, produces blood that may carry disease which harms and kills some recipients. Blood donation, *per contra*, produces blood that carries less disease which harms and kills fewer patients, and therefore is less dysfunctional than paid blood. But donation *alone* does not produce enough

* The risks are discussed in Part II.

blood, on which ground it is more dysfunctional than blood selling, or selling to supplement giving. The functionalist who postulates that blood donation is indispensable is dangerously wrong. There is usually a variety of means which fulfil a given function, nor need we choose between them as though they were mutually exclusive.

An alternative approach

Our criticism of what has been termed 'naïve functionalism' suggests an alternative version of functionalism that would be less 'naïve' and hence not subject to these fallacies. In short, it would not postulate that a given institution is necessary or even uniquely necessary for a specified function, nor would it over-simplify reality by postulating a single and overriding goal or social objective. The alternative would clearly be a form of functionalism which, when faced with a phenomenon for explanation, asked not 'Why does this phenomenon exist? but 'Why does this one exist rather than any other?' In its prescriptive form it would ask 'How important are our objectives relative to one another?', 'Which institutions are most functional for each objective?', and 'How dysfunctional are some institutions for objectives other than those for which they are functional?'

Titmuss's alternative tended to make the ideal the enemy of the good, which denies the propriety of these questions. In the world we know, these choices have to be made but *not* subject to a single and overriding ethical rule, The real problem in acknowledging that altruism may be a proper objective of social policy is whether it requires the example of generosity for it to be cultivated and to grow. Unfortunately few social scientists, if any, seem to have addressed themselves to this question. Titmuss certainly did not. We simply do not know how altruism is fostered, despite thousands of years of persuasion, proselytising and coercion. Even if we did, and people had not become perfectly altruistic, we would still need to find a compromise between fostering altruism to the maximum and getting other urgent jobs done that are no less worthy activities of man. Functionalist tunnel-vision would still be a social menace.

The alternative approach would take us out of the all-or-none world of moral absolutes and scientific naïveté into a more interesting intellectual realm capable of tackling the real world. The approach becomes an 'economic' approach in which costs and benefits corresponding to the dysfunctional and functional aspects of institutions are compared, given an hypothesised set of social objectives. This essay attempts to embody such an approach.

VI. GROUPS AND GIFTS

'All men, or most men, wish what is noble but choose what is profitable; and while it is noble to render a service not with an eye to receiving one in return, it is profitable to receive one.'

ARISTOTLE
Nichomachian Ethics

Familial giving

Under this head we briefly consider presents within families. This phenomenon appears to be perfectly consistent with pure altruism. With this type of giving, as with many others, a major preoccupation of the donor is to choose the gift which, out of the possibilities open to him, is most highly valued by the recipient—insofar as the donor can tell. It will be a relatively rare occurrence, and probably one accompanied by social disapproval, to find givers giving presents because they feel the gift they have selected is particularly meritorious, i.e. even though the recipient may not want it as much as some other (possibly of equal exchange value) he ought to have it because the *donor* regards it as good for him. This type of giving, in which an integral part of the gift relationship consists of a game of guessing the recipient's preferences, characterises the majority of gift acts associated with birthdays, namedays, Christmas, weddings.

The importance of the guessing-game must not be under-estimated. It might be argued that to be sure the gift was *really* that most preferred by the recipient the simplest method would be to give him a generalised commodity representing purchasing power, e.g. money. Money, however, is frequently (though not invariably) not the socially accepted form for the gift, because it fails (usually, though again not invariably) to demonstrate that substantial thought has gone into the choice of gift. (The desire to please family and closest friends frequently extends to a request for a list of gifts they would like, especially where the opportunity for studying their wants is limited and the 'guessing-game' has a high probability of going wrong.) Evidence that substantial thought has been put in is evidence that the giver cares about the person receiving the gift. In short, present-giving among close friends and relations is a means of cementing loving relationships—it is an outward and visible sign of an inward and spiritual relationship. There is substantial evidence that this is a valid interpretation of familial gift-relationships. The major evidence is the implicit moral obligation placed upon the recipient not to exchange the gift (unless it is explicitly removed by the donor). An exception to this rule is the gift of tokens and vouchers—such as record tokens—where the giver guesses that the recipient would wish the objects purchasable with the voucher but cannot be sure which object would please him most. It thus shows more 'care' than the gift of money. An embargo on exchange is, of course, perfectly consistent also with the 'meritoriousness' approach to giving: if the object of the gift were to ensure that a meritorious gift were consumed by the recipient, non-exchangeability is a necessary condition.

Finally, even gifts so intimate as those we have been discussing need not invariably carry a zero price to the recipient. Not infrequently gifts entirely consistent with the interpretation here are not given entirely freely. The giver 'helps one out' with the purchase of some special, highly prized and often highly priced object, or a 'matching gift'[21] is made where the donor contributes a penny for every penny the recipient provides. Giving gifts which carry a positive though less than the market price is common. Gifts made on such terms are not evidence of lesser altruism than gifts made entirely 'free'.

Collective giving

Gifts between *individuals* who are intimately known to one another, or between whom an intimate relationship is being established, tend to have the characteristics described above. With *collective* giving the emphasis shifts. The 'guessing game' becomes less significant. What does become significant is '*need*'. If one individual wishes that another individual, or group, should have an entity they currently lack, or more of an entity of which they have too little, he often describes the others as having a '*need*' for, or for more of, it.

Such 'needs' typically have a characteristic which makes them suitably met by collective action: that large numbers of persons agree the 'need' exists. Meeting such 'needs' accordingly takes on the aspects of a *public* good—if one person meets the 'need' (as he sees it) of another there is a very high probability that others (beside the direct beneficiary) will agree the 'need' has been met. There is accordingly a strong inclination for them to leave it to others to

[21] I owe this useful term to Arthur Seldon.

meet the 'need'. They will benefit from the indivisible benefits of the *public good*, a 'juster society', without having to divert resources from their own (non-public) consumption to mitigate the 'need'. They get a 'free ride'. In such circumstances a serious shortage in the degree to which agreed 'needs' are met is clearly possible, so that all will lose.

Collective action, in which individuals club together—literally in a club, a charity or as a nation—and agree terms upon which they contribute resources to meet 'needs' (subscriptions, taxes) are an obvious method of coping with the 'free-rider' problem. But it is not the only way. Another method, frequently practised for localised and 'one-off' 'needs', is to provide *private* incentives for localised and public 'needs'. Raffles, tombolas and other 'unfair' gambles are well-established and familiar methods of overcoming, to a degree, the problem of financing collectively-felt 'needs'. Another time-honoured method is publicising the names of contributors and the sums contributed, as the public corridor walls of many of our older hospitals will testify. Medals for war heroes and badges and certificates for blood donors serve the same purpose.

Each of these methods of meeting collectively-felt 'needs' dilutes the purity of the inter-personal gift described above by making it conditional. Action through a club, or the state, dilutes the purity of the inter-personal gift by making one person's contribution (or tax) conditional upon another's contribution (or tax). Action through a fund-raising campaign with prizes makes contributions conditional upon the receipt of personal reward.

What collective action is 'enough'?

'The ideal must always float before the soul of the artist, whatever art he practices, only as an unattainable standard.'

WILHELM VON HUMBOLT
The Limits of State Action

What 'needs' do individuals commonly assert exist? It is, of course, not sufficient for an individual to call attention to himself or his family (etc.) as in 'need'. His state must also be judged 'needy' by those who will be able to do, or coerce others into doing, something about it. The empirical manner in which needs are interpreted has been plausibly explained by Professor J. M. Buchanan:

'The mere fact that some members of the community are poor does not, in and of itself, normally impose an external diseconomy on many of the remaining members. What does impose such an external diseconomy is the *way* that certain persons behave when they are poor. It is not the low income of the family down the street that bothers most of us; it is that the family lives in a dilapidated house and dresses its children in rags that imposes on our sensibilities.'[22]

'Need', according to this view, is largely a *specific* thing, i.e. associated with individual entities in individuals' sets of preferences. Hence we see subsidies for housing, health, education and so on. It is also probably conditioned by proximity (again an empirical assertion, not a value-judgement). As Mandeville tells us of pity in *The Fable of the Bees*,

'it comes in either at the Eye, or Ear, or both, and the nearer, and more violently the Object of Compassion strikes those Senses, the greater Disturbance it causes in us'.[23]

These motives, as well as the 'free-rider' problem, make it difficult to assess the effectiveness of much collective giving. Were the funds nationally collected for relief in Biafra, Turkey or Bangladesh as much as the British would have liked? People appeared to care, but they probably contributed less than they cared. If so, two possible reasons are suggested by the discussion so far. One is that the free-rider problem was not resolved satisfactorily. This was certainly so in the three catastrophes—no *quo's* of any kind were offered. The second is that individuals were able to give only general funds to be spent for general purposes. One of the tragedies of disasters is that the more remote they are normally the more the difficulty in enabling individuals to contribute to specified 'needs' of specified persons: a pound contributed may be spent 50–50 on children's milk and adults' vaccine where the contributor might prefer proportions of 80–20.

Further, the compassion individuals *say* they have may not amount to as much as they do have, for no one seeks to appear an unsympathetic cad. In this sense, one doubts whether collective and public gifts will ever be 'enough'.

A more subtle aspect is that individuals may feel the additional costs to them are too high relative to the importance to them of the

22 J. M. Buchanan, 'What Kind of Redistribution Do We Want?', *Economica*, May 1968, p. 189.

23 Bernard Mandeville, *The Fable of the Bees*, Penguin Books, 1970, p. 264.

further 'needs' that could be met by more generous giving. Under these circumstances, it is neither dishonest, nor is any imperfection in institutions implied, if a man says that another is in 'need' but that he will do nothing (more) about it. There is a profound element of truth in the old saw that the poor are always with us.

Changing motives for giving

These considerations help to shed light on some of the alleged deficiencies of collective giving. Consider the much criticised siting of many of the old British voluntary hospitals. It is common to hear the criticisms of (private) collective charity that these charitable hospitals were situated away from the main residential areas and were ill-distributed as between the regions. Population movements since construction may explain some of this 'maldistribution', but not all of it. Yet, if the founders were not stupid, this criticism amounts to no more than an assertion that the critics have a different set of priorities. The complaint is misdirected at private collective action. The complaint should be that the critic was not around to found voluntary hospitals where *he* wanted them. This false criticism of private collective action does not in any way imply that all criticisms are false, or that the voluntary hospitals were sited efficiently.

Collective gifts for collective objectives (such as social assertion, avoidance of war, propitiation of the gods) characterise the types of gift drawn from the anthropological literature (pp. 35–37), and there is likewise no reason for criticising them on the grounds that few of us share the priorities, the beliefs, or the circumstances of primitive peoples. It is, however, entirely consistent with the praxeological approach that, as priorities or technologies change, the form and function of giving should also change. (National pride may attach to other qualities than the ability to destroy great wealth or to obligate debtor nations or tribes. War is most efficiently avoided in the age of cheap communication—and multi-contacts with foreign nations—by regular communication between rulers.)

In all these things, our theory cannot tell us whether what is, is right, or what is enough. It can sometimes tell us what institutions are more likely to approximate to the ideal. And it warns us against drawing naïve conclusions, whether moral or behavioural, from the evidence.

Spurious gifts

'Though I bestow all my goods to feed the poor, and have not charity, it profiteth me nothing.'

St. Paul to the Corinthians

A pure gift is a *quid* made with no conditional *quo*. A collective gift is characteristically, but by no means necessarily, a *quid* with an ancillary *quo*—it is a sharing agreement. In this section we investigate a type of spurious giving: *quids* that are extorted.

Since generosity, as distinct from altruism, is a behavioural phenomenon, it is evidently possible that much generous behaviour is not altruistic. One class of such behaviour is a *quid* given for a carefully hidden, or at least not an obvious, *quo*. People who 'scratch backs' clearly fall into this category. So does a good deal of other behaviour ranging from primitive giving recorded in the anthropological literature to moral blackmail. This form of spurious giving is relatively familiar and is probably not of much importance in social policy.

A form of spurious giving that is important is likely to be encountered with many forms of collective action. It will not be found in the 'club' where only the givers are represented and so will not normally be found in charity organisations.[24] But the possibility of 'gift extortion' arises with collective giving organised through the state. Gift extortion is not a phenomenon to be expected in voluntary charities because if their collective decision, no matter how reached, departs too radically from the wishes of a contributing member he may withdraw.

With collective giving that individuals have agreed to operate through the state, however, the presence among the membership (electorate) of those *to whom* collective gifts are made creates two conditions for gift extortion. Since the costs of leaving the territory governed by the state are enormously higher than those of leaving smaller collectivities, and the rules by which collective decisions are reached are much less often consensus than majority rules, it becomes possible for some sectors of society that gain a majority to vote for 'gifts' (transfers, benefits, etc.) to themselves. This process is precisely the opposite of the gift: instead of individuals giving voluntarily out

---

[24] Which is not to say that they do not have disadvantages. A frequently asserted one is that they are too small to operate as efficiently as they might, especially when several rival charities compete in identifying and measuring 'needs'. The author, however, knows of no test of this empirical assertion.

of altruism other individuals are taking by compulsion out of selfishness. The costs of implementing authoritarian preferences, as defined, are often much lower in collective action through the state—which is why authoritarians typically seek extensions to the power of the state while liberals seek to minimise it.[25]

Specific or general gifts and welfare economics

Liberals and economists espousing the conventional Pareto criterion (footnote 11, p. 42) have commonly preferred collective gifts, or transfers, in generalised purchasing power (money) to gifts in kind. The liberal argument is, broadly, that gifts of money maximise the beneficiary's freedom of choice and constrain the power of the givers over him to compel him to behave as *they* wish. They also advocate an equalisation of economic power because of the political power that often accompanies it. The welfare economics argument is that by giving the individual cash (or a *tradeable* gift in kind) he can probably attain a more preferred position than if he is given an untradeable gift in kind.

Our analysis of the economics of gift-relationships suggests that if the object of choice of the giver is a *specific* gift to an individual or group, as it very frequently is, then to award only *generalised* gifts, which may be spent in ways undesired by the giver, is to frustrate him. And normally, if the original transfer was sufficient to finance a specific gift desired by him, it will *reduce* the amount of the transfer. This is especially likely if the givers are better organised collectively than the recipients, for it will then be difficult for them to come to terms or make it politically unprofitable for a democratic politician to devise a better scheme by speculating about what the mutually agreeable terms might have been.

Secondly, if the giver's preferred gift is specific, *efficiency* will require a specific gift. It is then no longer necessary to dismiss as 'irrational' or as a 'mistake' the wide prevalence of gifts in kind handled through the agency of the state, a characteristic conclusion reached by economists who examined transfers from the point of view of the *recipient* only and concluded that, since cash transfers gave him a wider choice than transfers in kind, the former would enable him to reach a more preferred and hence more efficient

[25] Persons adopting the expanded Pareto criterion (footnote 11, p. 42) would judge each case on its merits and would not have any *general* prejudice about the role of the state. Such persons seem, alas, to be rare.

position. The economic functionalist approach identifies the function of giving as being one means of giving expression to the altruistic impulses of the givers. Hence, efficiency is achieved by the institution which most effectively enables them to reveal these impulses (so long as recipients are not harmed thereby).

The scope for specific gifts is limited, however, both by conventional *mores* and by technology. We have already suggested that familial giving tends to be characterised by a social convention that gifts should not normally be traded, and thus that donors must take care not to duplicate the gifts of others. In this case, specific gifts tend to be the rule. This convention does not apply in collective giving, and specific gifts tend therefore to be restricted to where technology prevents or restricts retrading. Thus if a person would rather have one pound's worth of beer than one pound's worth of coal, there is little point in giving him the coal one thinks he 'needs', for he can, if he chooses, readily exchange it for cash and thence for beer (ignoring transaction costs), unless one is willing to advocate making specified levels of coal consumption legally enforceable. By contrast, free health care to the sick, or free education, cannot be retraded in this way—at least, not if they are universally available, to all who choose to have them, at zero charge.

As an illustration of the potential fruitfulness of the approach, the economics of giving explains most of the key features of the British National Health Service: free care rather than discriminatory subsidies to the poor; its co-existence with private practice; its universalism. Similarly, the approach explains, at the more general level, why the general pattern of public taxation and expenditure is progressive.[26]

VII. CONCLUSION

'Science takes cognizance of a *phenomenon*, and endeavours to discover its law; art proposes to itself an *end*, and looks out for means to effect it.'

JOHN STUART MILL

Essays on Some Unsettled Questions of Political Economy (1844)

This essay set out only to indicate how a systematic economic

[26] On the health service, Cotton M. Lindsay, 'Medical Care and the Economics of Sharing', *Economica*, November 1969, and A. J. Culyer, 'Medical Care and the Economics of Giving', *Economica*, August 1971. On general redistribution, Harold M. Hochman and James D. Rodgers, 'Pareto Optimal Redistribution', *American Economic Review*, September 1969, pp. 542–557.

approach may be able to illuminate important social phenomena, to indicate the dangers and weaknesses in the naïve functionalist approach, and to show that the strictures that have defined the phenomena discussed as 'non-economic' have, for the most part, been misplaced. In short, we have sought to defend von Mises's apothegm and even have gone beyond his view of the economic realm—beyond what he termed 'catallactics'.

Unfortunately, even the friends of economic analysis place unwarranted bounds upon it. Even Professor P. M. Blau, in his stimulating application of economics to sociological phenomena, writes:

> 'In contrast to economic commodities, the benefits involved in social exchange do not have an exact price in terms of a single quantitative medium of exchange' and 'only social exchange tends to engender feelings of personal obligation, gratitude and trust; purely economic exchange as such does not.'[27]

Not surprisingly, Titmuss, who mistrusted economics and economists alike, reported the economic approach as neglecting

> 'large areas of gift actions and behaviour in both personal and impersonal contexts which do not involve physical objects, which are difficult or impossible to price and quantify in economic terms, and which, while involving an act of giving, carry no explicit right, expectation or moral enforcement of a return gift . . . such actions . . . have no exchange value.'[28]

It may be that *economists* have been slow to study such aspects of human behaviour but it does not follow that *economics* is emasculated.

The absence of an identifiable medium of exchange is no impediment to economic analysis. The absence of a unique or even positive price is not only consistent with, but implied by, the theory. The presence or absence of physical objects whose physical or value dimensions are 'quantifiable' is an irrelevance; so is what might be termed 'selfish' motives for giving, all of which may be incorporated into the analysis.

What, then, characterises the 'purely' economic? If non-contractual gift-relationships between strangers are incorporated into economic analysis, what is excluded? To describe a thing by what it is not would be an arduous task, but it is certainly possible to identify a key frontier against which an economic assault appears to be ineffectual. This is a problem that is at the core of the ethical views of Mauss and Titmuss on gifts. In the words of Mauss:

---

[27] P. M. Blau, *Exchange and Power in Social Life*, Wiley, New York, 1967, p. 94.
[28] Titmuss, *op. cit.* p. 212.

'We should return to the old and elemental. Once again we shall discover those motives of action still remembered by many societies and classes: the joy of giving in public, the delight in generous artistic expenditure, the pleasure of hospitality in the public or private feast.'[29]

Economics can give little if any guidance on how to make men altruistic but neither, it turns out, can Mauss or Titmuss. Instead we are offered the Rousseauesque prospect of the 'old and elemental'—presumably with everyone sleeping naked under his isolated oak!

However, and this is significant, if economics says little about altruism it can tell us how to make men (more) generous. The central and unresolved question must remain: in so adjusting social institutions to promote the generosity of man to man, is something lost? In attaining one social good do we destroy another, possibly higher, good? And even if we do not destroy it, to what extent can we tolerate its erosion? By making men free to sell *or* give, instead of only to give, we may increase generosity even though altruism remains the same. But, in the long—perhaps not so long—run, could it be that altruism needs the example of pure giving for it to be sustained? Suppose it did, and suppose also that selling *with* pure giving redistributed more things in the directions we may wish than pure giving without prices alone could do, how far would we sacrifice altruism for redistribution, or redistribution for altruism? The problem is again a praxeological one—a choice, but one for society as a whole, since it concerns society as a whole.

What the *right* action is can never be a question solely for the social scientist, for it must be determined ultimately by the aims and ambitions of society as a whole—of whom the scientist is but one, humble and ignorant. As Mill wrote:

'If, therefore, Political Economy be a science, it cannot be a collection of practical rules; though, unless it be altogether a useless science practical rules must be capable of being founded upon it.'[30]

Rules, therefore, for making a nation better are not science, but they depend upon the results of science. Perhaps the first of these is that all that glisters is not gold: noble acts can serve ignoble purposes, just as less noble motives can promote noble ends. Economics,

---

[29] Marcel Mauss, *op. cit.* p. 67.

[30] John Stuart Mill, *Essays on Some Unsettled Questions of Political Economy* (1844), reprinted by the LSE, Parker, London, 1948, p. 124.

or praxeology, does not of itself show how to make a nation 'good'; but whoever would be qualified to operate a social policy or to judge of the means of creating social justice and of liberating the noble soul from his base self, must first, if our arguments are correct, be a political economist. My (extreme) view is that the academic may go no further than this first step—an austere prescription, perhaps, but based on the view that science cannot prescribe and the belief that social scientists should not use the glamour of an apparently scientific method to lend spurious authority to their own ethical views.

4. The Calculus of Philanthropy*

THOMAS R. IRELAND

Associate Professor of Economics, University of Missouri—St. Louis

* This paper is drawn from the author's doctoral dissertation. It has been anglicised for British readers. An early, longer version for American readers was published in *Public Choice*, Fall, 1969.

THE AUTHOR

THOMAS R. IRELAND is Associate Professor of Economics at the University of Missouri—St. Louis Born in 1942, he was educated at Miami University, Ohio (BA in economics) and the University of Virginia (PhD in economics). He has taught economics at several universities since 1965–66; his present post is a combined appointment at University of Missouri—St. Louis and Southern Illinois University.

Professor Ireland specialises in public finance and public choice, is author (with David B. Johnson) of *The Economics of Charity* (Center for the Study of Public Choice, Blacksburg, Virginia, 1970), and (with Jack Rutner) of *Principles of Macroeconomics and Money* (Dryden Press, 1973), as well as articles in learned journals.

He is married to Marilyn J. Ireland; they have two children.

I. 'PUBLIC' MOTIVES AND PRIVATE PREFERENCES

Economics is the science concerned with individuals as they allocate scarce resources among wants and needs. As individuals allocate money, time and effort to philanthropic causes, they are allocating resources in non-governmental, but public, goods.[1] Yet private interests, as in all human affairs, must intervene and have a significant effect on the goals and outcomes of philanthropic work and organisation. How do public and private motives combine in individual philanthropic action?

There is no such thing as a truly 'public' motive. All individuals serve their own interests as they see them at a point in time. They do so whether their motives are purely personal financial gain or to better the 'quality' of society as they see it. Each individual looks on social organisation with a view based on his own experience and perhaps inherited traits. No individual can gauge what is best for society except in terms of the limited amount of information known to him. His view of a good society is therefore necessarily slanted in the direction of his own concerns. Only God could know what is absolutely best for society. Men must deal in much more humble, limited scopes. Thus, what might be called a person's 'public' motive could more accurately be regarded simply as a broader private motive. Since no man can truly know what is best for society, when he is motivated to improve it, the improvement must be defined by his own social preferences, essentially a normal part of his 'utility function'.[2] And since there is no true consensus about the nature of the good society, it is not possible to use such a concept to criticise the motives of men as they seek their interests. But, while it is beyond human scope ever to know with certainty how broadly a man is considering the good of society in contrast to direct personal aggrandisement, it is possible and valuable to distinguish between

[1] Public goods are goods the consumption of which by one individual does not reduce the quantity available for consumption by others, i.e. their supply is indivisible. Thus they are goods normally supplied *collectively*, e.g. national defence, and financed out of national revenues (taxes). If they were not, the 'free-rider' problem (below) would arise. But not all are 'pure' public goods, however (cable TV and open-air band concerts have elements of public and private goods). Nor are all goods and services usually categorised as public goods provided solely by government (in the US there are private police forces in addition to government police; in Britain private security firms supply essentially similar services).

[2] Mathematical relationships which link utility (preference) to quantity. These relationships are expressed as changes in marginal utility, i.e. the (small) amount of one good that would be given up for a larger quantity of another.

types of human motivation in philanthropic action. This is the purpose of the present short essay.

Each individual knows from his personal experience, and indeed from his inner conflicts, that men have to choose between broader social interests and more personal interests. Men are (other things equal) concerned that society shall be qualitatively improved for others, even when the change cannot easily be seen to benefit themselves. In a civilised society people are 'concerned' about the welfare of other people. And this concern, at least in some, leads to a type of behaviour defined as 'philanthropic'. But it is not as simple as that. It is not enough for an individual to have philanthropic concerns to behave in a philanthropic manner. Moreover men often behave in a philanthropic manner when they lack philanthropic concerns. To understand this proposition, it is helpful to think about the basic paradox of public finance—the 'free-rider' problem.[3]

The 'free rider'

When a 'public good' is merely indivisible, both in the 'pure' Samuelsonian sense[4] and in the 'imperfect' sense being developed by Professor J. M. Buchanan[5] and other public finance theorists, each individual will tend to avoid personal expenditure on it in the hope that others will make the necessary expenditure to provide it. In short, individuals will tend to try to take a 'free ride' at the expense of neighbours. This hypothesis is easily illustrated in the familiar and classic lighthouse situation. Every individual on an island would like a lighthouse constructed, but each attempts to avoid personal expenditure for its construction in the hope that others will pay for it. The result is that the lighthouse is not constructed, or is constructed in a less than efficient manner.[6]

---

[3] The 'free rider' as an idea in economic theory has been evolved largely by American economists in recent years. Its important implications for public goods analysis first appear in Paul A. Samuelson, 'The Pure Theory of Public Expenditure', *Review of Economics and Statistics*, 1954.

[4] Paul A. Samuelson, *ibid.*

[5] *The Demand and Supply of Public Goods*, Rand McNally, 1968.

[6] Efficiency here should be defined as provision of the public good up to the point at which

$$MC_s = \sum_i ME_i$$

where MC_s is the marginal social cost or expenditure on the good and $\sum_i ME_i$ is the sum of the marginal evaluations of individuals in the society for an additional unit of social expenditure on the public good.

The situation may not be changed when the public good is helping the 'needy' or providing a boys' club. Philanthropic activity may not be involved in either case. By moving from lighthouses to boys' clubs, no new elements have been added to the problem. Boys' clubs and lighthouses may both be regarded as public goods, even though in contemporary American and British society clubs are often provided through private philanthropic action and lighthouses through normal collective action. If philanthropic elements are ignored, the conditions for efficient action and decision-making problems are the same. Will the social decision process result in an efficient provision of boys' clubs or lighthouses?

While philanthropic action is normally directed at providing a public good, there are added elements in a philanthropic individual's motivation toward supplying the public good which change the efficiency conditions of the society for provision of the public good. It is necessary to discuss the motives leading to philanthropic action to explain how these changes take place.

II. MOTIVES FOR PHILANTHROPIC ACTION

There are five principal motives for philanthropic action:

(1) *A desire for public goods in terms of direct personal motives*
The individual desires the public good because of anticipated direct personal benefits to himself. Such a motive must help to explain an individual's decision to contribute funds toward cancer research, which may eventually help him. Likewise, an individual may contribute to family service, his church, or the Boy Scouts partly because of the expectation that he will directly benefit from them.

(2) *A desire for public goods in terms of broader public motives*
The motive may be to see others benefited: a neighbour helped in a crisis, retarded children cared for, old people made more comfortable, the ill-housed housed better, pain relieved, etc. This is not a truly philanthropic motive even though it involves a large degree of 'public-spiritedness' because it does not imply any necessary willingness to *act* to achieve the result. The individual has a desire to have a purpose accomplished, as in the directly personal public goods motive. The difference between the first and second motives is simply in the *reasons* why he wants the public good, not in the way in

which he would go about obtaining it. The free-rider problem is fully operative in each case.

(3) *A desire to* act *in a 'good' fashion*
This is the truly philanthropic motive: the individual desires to be the agent in a process of achieving a public good. The satisfaction achieved by operating under this motive comes from the process of acting and is related only indirectly to the result of the act. Normally the desire to act in a 'good' fashion will be coupled with a desire to achieve a public good for broader reasons, as in motive (2), but the relationship is not simple. The reason for the connection between the two motives is that in order to be able to act in a 'good' fashion, an individual must have some method of evaluating the act as good. Further, if he is to act other than randomly, he must have some method of selecting *priorities* among the 'good' acts he may choose to perform. Presumably, some 'good' acts are 'better' than others. It is on the basis of the result of 'good' actions that the individual determines the quality of, and satisfaction from, a 'good' act. But the satisfaction an individual receives from the result of his action, described in motive (2), is fundamentally different from the satisfaction he receives because he is the agent producing the result. He receives the satisfaction of the *result* no matter who provides it. He receives the satisfaction of the *act* only if *he* performs the act. There is no direct and fixed correlation between the 'goodness' of the act and the 'goodness' of its result. Some kinds of broader public goods lend more 'goodness' to each act of contributing a pound than others, even though the individual considers the result of the contributed pound to be equal. There is more 'goodness' for most persons in the act of providing toys for orphans than there is in providing an equally valued amount of yachting wharfs to yachting enthusiasts. There is probably also more 'good' in providing fruit baskets to old ladies at Christmas than in providing an equally valued amount of mosquito protection. The *type* of public good, in addition to its *value*, will determine the *act* satisfaction of providing the good.

The desire to *perform* a 'good' act, as separate from the *results* of the act, will hereafter be referred to as the 'Kantian' motive, after the German philosopher, Immanuel Kant. It is this motive which is necessary for philanthropic action (or pretences of it), and it is around this motive that conditions for efficient philanthropy will be developed. In seeking to define the quality of a 'good' or 'moral' act, Kant insisted that 'goodness' in an act required that the motivation for it must be divorced from all aspects of personal gain for the actor. In Kant's system, for an individual to commit a good act, he must derive no satisfaction from the purpose of the act, but do it only because he attributes the quality of goodness to it. This means that the individual must only do the act because he is motivated by the desire to act in a good fashion. In practice, it is difficult to imagine such purity of motivation. If the effect of the act is good, it is difficult not to derive some satisfaction from the result, and if the result is not good, it is difficult to imagine that the act which brought about the result was 'good'. For the purposes of this essay, therefore, it is inconvenient to insist on Kant's purity of motivation, but it is convenient to refer to the desire to commit a 'good' act as the Kantian motive.[7]

(4) *The political motive*

One of the first instructions given to an aspiring young politician is that he engage himself in work for charitable organisations to develop a 'non-partisan' reputation as a leader in his community before he attempts to seek elective office. Obviously philanthropic endeavour is not the only route into elective office, but it is a route commonly trod by politicians, especially in local elections.

Yet more is included under the political motive for philanthropic work than the desire of aspiring politicians to build an elective base. Politics among individuals includes far more than running for elective office. It includes the desire of individuals to advance in bureaucratic structures,[8] to maintain a position of prestige in a community and to influence the direction of community development, either for broader social or more directly personal reasons. Philanthropic endeavour often pleases superiors in a corporation or any other bureaucracy, because local élites, usually composed of corporate, labour and special interest organisation leaders, like to shape the direction of community development. Likewise, an individual may be using his philanthropic efforts to secure a specific personally desired public good, such as a road, or a public playground near his home. Working in charitable organisations, which tend to be controlled by local élites, is a means of rising in their favour. Prestige in a community and advancement in a bureaucratic structure depend, in

---

[7] Immanuel Kant, *Lectures on Ethics*, Harper and Row, Harper Torchbook edition, New York, 1963, pp. 27–33.

[8] Gordon Tullock, *The Politics of Bureaucracy*, Public Affairs Press, Washington DC, 1965.

large measure, on securing the favour of élites. Therefore individuals seeking either corporate advancement or community prestige or some specific governmental action are led to compete to gain the opportunity of providing personal effort to philanthropic organisation. This motive, in all its aspects, is central to charity budgeting as well as the private system of taxation developed for contributions to United Appeal funds (Appendix, pp. 75–78).

(5) *Condition-of-employment motive*
Contributions to philanthropic organisations, especially United Appeals, is often implicitly or explicitly a condition of employment in many companies and offices, both blue and white collar. Hence occasional management-labour conflicts. In such cases, individual contribution may be aimed solely at maintaining employment in a location, the level of required contributions varying from location to location. Often, of course, the effect of non-contribution is not outright dismissal, but rather resistances to advancement or simply harassment, such as requiring the employee to explain to his immediate superior why he did not contribute. The important economic aspect is that there is a specific amount by which an employee can prevent a 'bad' result.

III. ANALYSIS OF SOCIAL EFFICIENCY CONDITIONS

The public good motives

Any or all of the five motives may be involved in a decision to contribute. When motives (3), (4) and (5) are taken into account, the conditions for social efficiency become much more complicated than those described in footnote 6 for the public good motives. Both the desire for public goods in terms of direct personal motives and broader public motives generate normal demands for a public good. They raise no special questions in public goods theory.

The Kantian motive

In the Kantian motive, the act of contribution is itself a factor. The goal of a Kantian act is *act utility*, not the utility of the *result* the act brings about. What the individual derives satisfaction from is the *act* of doing the 'good' deed of providing the funds. The cost of the act is the foregone alternative uses of the funds given up. In this sense, the Kantian motive is not really a public goods motive but rather a desire for the private satisfaction of doing a 'good' deed. Yet this private satisfaction results in the provision of funds for public goods purposes. However, the amount of funds individuals seek to provide in this manner is not directly related to the amount they would seek to have in terms of the public goods motives. In the public goods motives, individuals seek the *result* of having public goods. In the Kantian motive, the individual seeks only the *act utility* of providing the goods. This dichotomy leads to the paradox that individuals might voluntarily contribute for the provision of a public good in excess of the amount of the public good which would be justified by non-Kantian efficiency conditions.[9]

When both types of motives are involved, the dichotomy between the sources of satisfaction in the Kantian and public goods motives greatly complicates the social efficiency conditions for the provision of public goods. At a given level of social expenditure on the public good, whether provided by tax or donation financing, the individual's marginal evaluation for one more unit will be the same regardless of the source of provision.[10] However, the individual's marginal Kantian satisfaction will depend directly on how much social expenditure he himself provides voluntarily. The sum of individual Kantian satisfactions therefore will depend on how much each individual has contributed, so that, for different combinations of individual contributions equalling the same total expenditure, the sum of Kantian satisfactions can vary. This implies that the source of the expenditure makes a difference to the society as a whole. This conclusion is in contrast to the public goods model in which the source of provision is only important to individuals as they bear the burden of taxes, but not in the efficiency conditions for society as a whole as long as no individual is made worse off.[11] The limit for such provision is described in footnote 6.

Efficiency conditions with Kantian elements

When individuals desire, in varying degrees, to be part of the

---

[9] Under certain complex conditions, a tax might be justified to reduce the amount of the public good provided under these circumstances.

[10] For the public goods motives, marginal satisfactions must be evaluated in a *numéraire* rather than in terms of satisfactions to be derived from some specific act of the individual. This is correctly stated as ME_p. For the Kantian motive, the marginal satisfaction is the marginal gain (or utility) derived from giving one more dollar toward the provision of the public good, which is correctly stated as MU_k.

[11] This will be true as long as the benefits to an individual from additional units of the public good exceed his tax cost for them. There are a large number of dispersions of the tax burden over infra-marginal ranges which will achieve this result, and each is equally efficient in the absence of the Kantian motive.

expenditure process because of the Kantian motive, the source of the funds for the purchase of the public good makes a significant difference. Therefore, deriving the analysis of the efficiency conditions for social allocation is made much more complex.

To begin the analysis of the new efficiency conditions, it is useful, for setting benchmarks, to construct a rather abstract model in which the Kantian motive is operative, but public goods created by Kantian acts are assumed to be of only negligible value (instances are difficult to imagine). Something must cause an individual to feel that certain acts are 'good'. The reason why most 'good' acts are evaluated as 'good' is that they bring about 'good' results, and 'good' results imply that the provision of the public goods is more than of negligible importance. Rather than conjure up an extreme example, it will simply be hoped that the reader will accept the abstraction.[12] In the abstract model thus created, each individual will continue contributing pounds to receive the satisfaction of doing a 'good' act up to the point at which the act satisfaction derived from giving one more pound is less than the satisfaction to be gained in alternative uses.[13] It is assumed that separate individual 'good' acts can be channelled through the common denominator of pounds of contribution into the provision of some public good. As suggested by Professor Buchanan,[14] if the 'good' act were, for some perverse reason, one of burning money, there is no way that one could speak of the collective good being provided. The assumption, however, that contributed pounds are being channelled into the provision of some public good follows almost necessarily from the analysis of this essay that virtually all 'good' acts are good because they cause 'good' results, in which event a public good of some sort is being provided.

Thus, some amount of public good will be provided by *voluntary* action, and this amount will be socially efficient, since there is no role for collective action in terms of the Kantian motive (because

12 Possibly, the recent practice by members of the Catholic faith of foregoing the eating of meat on Fridays is the nearest thing to a good example. Other near examples can also be found in religious activity, which is not a focus of this essay. [The 'Friday fish' practice of Catholics has become uncommon since the injunction was removed in the 1960s, which seems to suggest that the original motive was not Kantian.—ED.]

13 $\frac{M^u{}_k}{£1} = \frac{M^u{}_a}{£1} = \frac{M^u{}_b}{£1} = \ldots \frac{M^u{}_n}{£1}$,

where (a, b, c, . . ., n) is the set of all alternative uses of funds being allocated and MU_k is the Kantian satisfaction from using funds for 'good' acts.

14 J. M. Buchanan, in correspondence.

compulsory giving through taxation does not create the utility of doing a 'good' act). In other words, pounds raised through taxation yield no Kantian satisfactions.

When the public goods motives at more than negligible significance are re-introduced, the individual's incentive to contribute is stronger than in the absence of the public goods motives because he receives the *end utility* of enjoying the public good as well as the *act utility.* In evaluating whether to give an additional pound, however, the individual will be aware that, because of the 'free-rider' effect, his own contribution will make contributions by other individuals less likely. His act of contribution and consequent provision of units of the public good lowers the total marginal evaluations of other individuals for additional units, because marginal satisfactions from additional units diminish with increases in the quantity provided. This effect will mean that a contributing individual will assume that a contribution by himself of one pound will result in an increase in the total provision of the public good of less than a pound. He will assume that his own contribution of a pound will lower the contributions of other individuals by some amount since the total marginal evaluations of the public good will be lowered for other individuals, and that the contributions of other individuals will therefore be lowered by his own contribution, but by some amount less than a pound. In other words, the individual realises that if he increases his own contribution by one pound, other individuals will have more of the public good and smaller marginal evaluations of and incentives for still further additional units, but that this response by other individuals will cause them to reduce their contributions by something less than a pound. Therefore, the individual will take into account his marginal evaluation of whatever addition to the total provision of the public good his contribution will bring into being in deciding whether to contribute another pound.[15]

The political motive

The political motive is primarily dependent on the Kantian motive.

[15] It should be pointed out that a subsidy to increase provision of the public good beyond amounts voluntarily provided is justified by welfare criteria if the condition listed in footnote 6 is not met. The amount of the subsidy is not easily arrived at, however, since a government subsidy could reduce private contributions and hence replace expenditures from which Kantian satisfactions were derived with expenditures without Kantian satisfactions. Since this is true, a subsidy of £100 might increase the amount of provision of the public good by only, say, £80. In addition, Kantian satisfaction losses must be compensated in terms of welfare criteria.

The political desire is to appear to have done a 'good' act in order to impress other individuals favourably, for whatever reason is thought desirable. This is not to suggest that Kantian and political motives are not ordinarily mutually operative, nor that the political motive takes the form only of a desire to appear to be doing a 'good' act. A secondary political desire may be to develop 'contacts' by working in philanthropic organisations with politically powerful individuals. Nonetheless, the desire to impress the individuals is the primary part of the political motive, and a restatement of efficiency conditions will be attempted only in terms of that part of the motive.

Fortunately, the desire to act in a 'good' manner and to appear to have done so are closely related. Both motives focus on the desire to act, not the desire for the result. And they both differ from the public good motives because the amount of satisfaction derived depends directly on how much the individual has contributed, rather than on how much was finally provided. When an individual considers contributing one more pound, he considers that an additional pound of contributions will yield some additional Kantian and political satisfactions and some additional total provision of the public good. The amount of the addition will be something less than a pound because of the free-rider problem.

Condition-of-employment motive

The condition of employment motive differs from the others primarily because it involves a specific price which the individual can pay to avoid a 'bad' result. If the individual contributes a given amount, he will not be fired, or harassed, or barred from advancement, etc. This motive centres around a single sterling amount, the payment of which can enable the individual to avoid a bad result. Also, there is no relationship between the condition of employment motive and other motives except insofar as the individual suffers less from making the payment necessary to maintain employment if other motives are strong.

IV. SUMMARY AND CONCLUSIONS

When charitable elements are involved, many normal conclusions about the efficiency of government substitution for private market outcomes must be revised. There are psychic losses suffered by givers who in the private situation gained the satisfactions of good behaviour, but in the public situation are merely reluctant taxpayers. Such considerations are less important, to be sure, than the effects of the gifts on beneficiaries, but no good society has ever been judged solely by the quality of the beneficiaries of its transfers of income. Some concern should be given to the welfare of those who provide the transfers.

Appendix

Charity in North America: The United Fund

The North American institution of the United Fund illustrates the political and condition-of-employment motives for charitable activity described in the text.

A united fund (UF) is a local charitable organisation, usually centred in a metropolitan area. It acts as a fund-raising and distributing unit for charitable agencies that provide services in its area: welfare-oriented community service organisations such as Boy Scouts and similar youth-directed service organisations, neighbourhood planning, development and welfare units, ethnic-American or Canadian welfare units, private adoption agencies, orphans' homes, marriage guidance services, the Salvation Army and the Red Cross. It does not include the substantial charity activity in education, religion (although it is involved with religiously-affiliated welfare agencies), politics, and disease research and prevention. In recent years, the UF has consistently raised and disbursed funds amounting to about 0·1 per cent of personal income in both the United States and Canada (see Table).[1]

Each UF is an autonomous unit with no centralised direction or supervision in its fund-raising or fund-disbursing activities, although there is a national servicing organisation called the United Way of America (formerly United Community Funds and Councils of America) which acts primarily as an information-gathering and dispensing organisation with some research objectives. It has also a minor lobbying function with the Federal Government of the United States (in Canada the Canadian Welfare Council).

Within the UF movement there is a special emphasis of citizen non-professional control over the fund-raising and budgetary-allocational activities of a given group of organisations. Frequently the fund-raising organisations, usually called United Funds proper, are separate from the allocating ('community chest') organisation.

The chairman of a fund-raising campaign is likely to be a prominent corporate executive with good contacts with the local social élite. He and his committee will all be volunteers who must have the support of their corporate superiors (or stockholders) because of the time they will put into the fund-raising campaign. Allowing one of their executives to serve in such a position is a major charitable contribution of the corporation to the UF process that they are usually pleased

---

[1] Material from *Charity Budgeting*, my doctoral dissertation for the University of Virginia, 1968, or a condensation in *The Economics of Charity*, Public Choice Society, Blacksburg, Va., 1970.

TABLE: UNITED FUNDS AS FRACTIONS OF GNP AND PERSONAL INCOME: USA AND CANADA, SELECTED YEARS, 1920 TO 1966

	Total UF USA & Canada $million	UF/USA $million	UF/Canada $million	UF/GNP USA	UF/GNP Canada	% GNP Can.–USA	UF/PI USA	UF/PI Canada	% PI Can.–USA
1920	19·6			0·00021			0·00025		
1930	76·0			0·00079			0·00093		
1940	86·4	82·3	4·1	0·00084	0·00060	0·714	0·000105	0·00082	0·780
1945	221·3	213·8	7·5	0·00101	0·00063	0·623	0·00125	0·00082	0·656
1950*	193·2	183·0	10·2	0·00064	0·00056	0·882	0·00080	0·00076	0·950
1955	302·0	286·0	16·0	0·00072	0·00059	0·819	0·00092	0·00081	0·880
1960	458·2	428·9	29·4	0·00085	0·00081	0·952	0·00107	0·00107	1·000
1965	584·6	544·9	39·7	0·00080	0·00076	0·950	0·00102	0·00102	1·000
1966	625·5	582·6	43·0	0·00079	0·00074	0·936	0·00100	0·00101	1·001

*The figures for Canada in 1950 are averages of two figures provided by the Canadian Welfare Council.

Sources: UCFCA, *1966 Directory*, New York; United Fund totals for Canada provided by Canadian Welfare Council; *Canada Year Book*, 1968; *Economic Report of the President*, 1967.

to make because his public relations value to the corporation will be considerably enhanced.

Giving becomes a condition of employment

The fund-raising campaign will have the support of virtually all leaders in the community. Many corporations apply so much pressure on their employees to give that giving in effect becomes a condition of employment. The media provides free advertising in regular reports on how close the campaign is to its goal. There will also be much paid advertising of the campaign, frequently at reduced advertising rates. The direction and control of this campaign will ultimately be in the hands of volunteer unpaid citizens of the community.

The budgetary-allocational side of the UF process will be less glamorous. The budget committees' members will not receive as much favourable publicity as the fund-raising committee. The work itself will be less creative and the decisions made less satisfying.

Advantages of the United Fund system

To the individual contributor, the fund as a system for charitable allocations offers several advantages. To corporations, which contribute 40 per cent of UF total income, the advantage is in making one contribution rather than several or many to individual agencies that might otherwise solicit contributions. A UF shifts the determination of the quality of appeals to experts of the same background and interests as the corporate executives.

For its employees, the UF provides another advantage to a corporation. It solicits employees primarily at their place of employment. One campaign is usually permitted by the corporation because campaigns consume employee work-time.

The UF protects the individual (non-corporate) contributor from multiple solicitations at the place of employment, and to some extent against fraudulent solicitations. He is still solicited at home for contributions by disease fighting, educational and political agencies, but the volume of charity requests is at least reduced. He is also provided the opportunity to give without having to make careful evaluations of where and in what proportions he would like his money distributed. (He is in some cases permitted to earmark his contributions for particular agencies, though earmarking is not normally allowed to influence the total size of agency allocations by the budget committee. In practice, the total amount given to any agency is far larger than the amount earmarked for it. Thus, earmarking by individuals is in effect ignored.)

Economies of scale in the fund-raising process mean that a larger proportion of money is given by individuals and corporations than they would give if each agency did its own solicitations. Much less is spent on advertising per unit of monies raised, and fewer resources are devoted to solicitation generally. The proportion of US charity funds used to finance fund-raising may rise as high as 60 per cent in small non-fund affiliated charities. In funds themselves, this figure is 3 per cent as a national average (although it places no value on volunteer manpower services that are a true cost).

Why are United Funds peculiar to North America?

Thus, it would seem that, on a number of grounds, United Funds are efficient institutions for fund-raising—a kind of social but non-governmental control over private welfare and private giving. And yet it is an institution common only to the US and Canada. Almost every metropolitan area in the US and Canada has its UF. This is not true of any other country in the world. The idea has been tried elsewhere: in 1966, there were two funds in the Philippines, one in Australia and one in South Africa, but it has simply not caught on elsewhere in the sense that it has become dominant in the US and Canada.

Why? Canada's form of government is far closer to those of Britain, Australia and New Zealand than to the US. Her public welfare institutions are also more clearly similar to other nations in the British Commonwealth than the US. Her rate of growth has been much faster than that in the US since the First World War when the UF developed in both countries. The basic inter-connectedness of the American and Canadian economies may be a partial explanation, but each fund is local in character. It cannot simply be a common border: Mexico does not have United Funds. It is not urbanisation: Canada is much more rural than the US.

There are no simple answers, which makes the parallel development of the institution in both countries even more striking. The first true United Fund was organised in Cleveland, Ohio, in 1913 (although a prototype existed in Denver, Colorado, as early as 1887). The first Canadian fund was organised in Montreal in 1918, a lapse of a mere five years. In the same year (1918), the 21 existing United Funds organised the American Association for Community Organisations, which after several name changes is now the United Way of America, as mentioned earlier. From that start, the inter-connectedness of the development of United Funds in the two countries has been so complete that although the total funds for the US *plus* Canada are available since 1920, they cannot now be disaggregated into American and Canadian totals for the period from 1920 to 1939. Comparative data for the period from 1940 to 1966, broken down into totals for each country, is presented in the Table.[2] This information and its implications for similarities in UF contribution patterns in the two countries is best shown in the last column, where the fraction of aggregate personal income given to United Funds in Canada is divided by the same fraction in the US. It may be purely coincidental, but the fraction of personal income given to the funds in the two countries was identical in five of the years from 1945–1966. In three other years the difference was only one-tenth of 1 per cent.

Again, the question remains: Why? How could a local form of charitable organisation grow up in two and only two countries with really quite different characters, especially in forms of government and dominant social problems, even as handled by the funds themselves? How could the fractions of their incomes they devote to one particular type of charitable activity be so similar?

---

2 Data reproduced from tables in *The Economics of Charity*, *op. cit.*

5. The Charity Market: Theory and Practice

DAVID B. JOHNSON

Associate Professor of Economics,
Lousiana State University

'To distinguish that which is chivalrous and noble from that which is not, is a task that needs care and thought and labour; and to perform that task is a first duty for economists . . .'

ALFRED MARSHALL
'Social Possibilities of Economic Chivalry', *Economic Journal* (1907)

THE AUTHOR

DAVID B. JOHNSON is 33, was educated at Marquette University and the University of Virginia (PhD in Economics, 1968), and has been Associate Professor of Economics at Louisiana State University since 1967. In 1974 he will take up a one-year appointment as senior international research economist at the US Treasury.

His publications include *The Economics of Charity* (with Thomas Ireland), Public Choice Society (1970), and articles in *Economica* and the *Journal of Law and Economics*.

I. INTRODUCTION

However chivalrous the motivations or the outcome of individual decision-making, a differentiating characteristic of man is that he selects or chooses among ends and means to ends. Man individually on an island is confronted with physical constraints, but his decisions are personal and are not confined by social institutions. When he is joined by millions of other individuals few, if any, choices are purely personal; most are made within the framework of a social institution. Traditional economic analysis has examined the choices of man disciplined only by nature, perhaps joined by one partner, and the human choices made within an economic or private market mechanism. More recently, to borrow Professor Kenneth Boulding's terms,[1] we have been witnessing the entry of economic 'imperialism' into such previously isolated disciplines as sociology, political science, psychology, law, etc., and economics is rapidly becoming a discipline which studies individual-choice behaviour and its consequences in social institutions other than the private market.

The recent debate on blood supply and allocation between the late Professor R. M. Titmuss and Messrs. Michael Cooper and Anthony Culyer is an extension of economic imperialism into yet another commodity (blood) and mechanism (the gift relationship).[2]

There are at least three main market institutions in which individual choices are made and resources procured and allocated:

(1) the *private* market, in which individuals produce and allocate private goods through separate but integrative personal decisions guided by the price mechanism;

(2) the *political* market, in which individuals collectively decide on the provision and allocation of public goods and then selectively enforce their decisions by penalties; and

(3) the *charity* market, in which individuals 'voluntarily' and collectively provide public goods.

Various combinations of the three exist in practice. While the most interesting and productive research may lie in studying their combinations, it is instructive to examine each at its polar limit.

[1] 'Economics as a Moral Science', *American Economic Review*, March 1969.

[2] R. M. Titmuss, 'Ethics and Economics of Medical Care', *Medical Care*, Vol. I. No. 1, 1963; *Choice and the Welfare State*, Fabian Tract 370, 1967; *The Gift Relationship*, Allen and Unwin, London, 1970; Michael Cooper and Anthony Culyer, *The Price of Blood*, Hobart Paper 41, Institute of Economic Affairs, 1968. The debate is continued in Part II of this *Readings*.

A. The Private Market

The mechanics of the private market and its dominant mechanism the price system have been formalised into a well-integrated conceptual framework; their strengths and weaknesses are well known. The pricing system serves as a communicative device between and among producers and consumers and as an inducement device to reward people who make efficient choices. It is unequalled by any other mechanism in providing efficient production and allocation of private goods. By providing a wide range of alternatives, it is compatible with a high degree of individual freedom in consumption, location, and employment, and there is some reason to believe that its existence is a necessary condition for long-run political freedom.[3] Not least, the private market permits charitable preferences to be acted out (pp. 88–90).

Critics dislike the private market for diverse reasons:

(1) individuals make choices which the critics do not believe should be made;

(2) the market system does not 'internalise' all costs and benefits;[4]

(3) the critics do not approve of the market's income (wealth) distribution, which is a result of the number and type of resource units owned, and their use;

(4) the market is beset by too many impediments, such as ignorance of alternatives, monopolistic elements, etc.;

(5) the private market debases the natural goodness of man.[5]

---

[3] Professor F. A. Hayek, among others, has been a leading supporter of the thesis that a private market is necessary to ensure political freedoms. The most thorough presentation of his views is in *The Constitution of Liberty*, Routledge and Kegan Paul and University of Chicago Press, 1960.

[4] Costs and benefits are not 'internalised' when the decision-making unit does not bear the costs or receive the benefits of its actions. A manufacturing firm which dumps its by-products into a stream which requires a downstream firm or municipal water system to purify the water is not internalising all of the costs in its production process. Air pollution by steel mills is another widely cited example. These examples do not constitute an effective criticism of the private market because the resources involved are common and not private property and some of the worst offenders, in the United States and probably other countries, are local, state and federal political units.

[5] These criticisms of the private market are discussed in most modern economic principles texts, a typical example of which is Paul Samuelson's *Economics*, 8th edn., McGraw-Hill, 1970. The argument that the private market debases the natural goodness of man is most forcefully stated in Titmuss, *The Gift Relationship*, *op. cit.* Criticisms of the private market by members of the 'New Left' are discussed in Assai Lindbeck's *The Political Economy of the New Left*, Harper and Row, 1971. An excellent evaluation of

B. The Political Market

Even if the private market produced and allocated private goods to the satisfaction of all citizens, there would remain a compelling argument for the political market to provide 'public goods', defined as providing benefits from which individuals cannot be excluded and of which one man's consumption does not decrease the amount available to other men.

The classic example of a public good is national defence. John benefits from having one additional nuclear submarine stationed as a deterrent without decreasing the benefits to George. Also, John cannot be easily excluded from the benefits provided by the submarine and therefore, it is argued, private firms could not package and sell the defence services of submarines because they could not exclude from its benefits individuals who refused to pay for them. Similarly, voluntary or charitable contributions would fall short of providing the optimal amount of defence: the rational man would refuse to contribute even if he had a high preference for defence because he would reason (correctly) that his individual contribution would have no perceptible effect on the provision of the nuclear submarine. The 'free rider' has become the basic analytical argument for a political market, or government, in a society of free individuals.

A political market is essential to provide the framework in which citizens can collectively decide on the type and quantities of public goods they want and in which penalties, such as fines or imprisonment, can be enforced for those who attempt a free ride. The actual or potential enforcement of these penalties constitutes the *sine qua non* of the political market. Without such penalties individuals could vote for the provision of a public good and then attempt a free ride, hoping that George would finance it; George, of course, would be reasoning similarly.

Economists refrained from investigating the political market until less than two decades ago, but they have more recently begun applying their tools intensively. Unfortunately, there remains a fundamental analytical asymmetry between the theoretical treatment of the political market and that of the private market. A theory receives effective criticism only when it is explicitly developed and is well known. Private market price theory has been subjected to considerable

---

these criticisms is contained in Alchian and Allen, *University Economics*, 3rd edn., Wadsworth, 1972 (an adaptation of the section on 'Philanthropy' is included in this *Readings* as Essay No. 1, pp. 3–13).

criticism, whereas the political market, devoid of an integrative theoretical framework, has received little substantive criticism.

C. The Charity Market

Although there is a third, charity, market in which individuals collectively provide public goods without the incentives or penalties of the political market, virtually no research has been directed to it.[6]

Perhaps this neglect, or at least the lack of theoretical development, can be explained by the restrictive interpretation economists have placed on the meaning of 'rational man'. According to the usual interpretation, a rational man will not voluntarily contribute to the provision of a public good because of the 'free-rider' problem; his single contribution would have no perceptible effect on its provision, and he could not be excluded from its benefits. Hence, the charity market as a mechanism for financing and allocating resources has, by definition, been eliminated from the scope of economic analysis. But once it is recognised that rational men may be motivated by goals or incentives not generally considered in this narrow version of *homo economicus*, such as social pressure, religion, etc., the charity market can be analysed by the tools of theoretical economics and applied political economy.

Charity is the 'voluntary'[7] transfer of income or goods below the market price from one individual to another or to an intermediary agency. Welfare transfers may be charitable and such transfers are employed in this essay to illustrate the economics of charity. However, welfare transfers occur through the political market as well as through the charity market; a person voluntarily contributing to national defence can be said to be charitable, but we would not classify these contributions as welfare.[8]

An analytical distinction must also be made between 'collective' and 'personal' charity. 'Wholesale' charity implies an intermediary which solicits and collects funds from donors and distributes them

[6] In 1971, Americans allocated $21·15 billion, 2·04 per cent of personal disposable income, through it: *Giving, U.S.A.*, American Association of Fund Raising Counsel, 1971. Further discussion of a part of the charity market, for blood, in the US is in my essay (No. 3) in Part II.

[7] As used in this essay, 'voluntary' means the absence of the use (or threat of use) of legal or illegal coercive power by the state or of illegal coercion by other individuals.

[8] Welfare provision has many of the characteristics of a pure public good except that it is divisible. A single individual may not be able to eradicate all poverty, but he might be able to alleviate the poverty of one or two families.

to other intermediaries or to beneficiaries.* 'Personal' charity incorporates direct person-to-person contact, such as giving food or money to a needy neighbour. This distinction is important because the motivations and efficiency of the two kinds vary, and increased urbanisation has shifted the mix in favour of the collective. Thomas R. Malthus had some comments relevant to this dichotomy and to our analysis below:

'In the great charitable institutions supported by voluntary contributions, some of which are certainly of a prejudicial tendency, the subscriptions, I am inclined to fear, are sometimes given grudgingly, and rather because they are expected by the world from certain stations and certain fortunes, than because they are prompted by motives of genuine benevolence; and as the greater part of the subscribers do not interest themselves in the management of the funds or in the fate of the particular objects relieved, it is not to be expected that this kind of charity should have any strikingly beneficial influence on the minds of the majority who exercise it. . . .

'But it is far otherwise with that voluntary and active charity, which makes itself acquainted with the objects which it relieves; which seems to feel, and to be proud of the bond that unites the rich with the poor; which enters into their houses, informs itself not only of their wants, but of their habits and dispositions; . . .'[9]

II. PRELIMINARY ECONOMIC ANALYSIS OF THE CHARITY MARKET

A. Personal Welfare Charity

Economists use two-person models—say, Able and Baker—to illuminate certain features of private market trading. This simple device can also be employed in understanding the terminology and analysis of personal charity, i.e. where the giver (Able) directly confronts the taker (Baker).†[10]

Merely assuming that Able is not a purely 'economic man' and that he is concerned about the welfare of Baker is not a sufficient

* [An American example is the United Funds, described in this *Readings* by Professor Thomas Ireland in the Appendix to Essay No. 4, pp. 75–78. A selection of statistics on the sources and allocation of US private and corporate charity is given in the Appendix to this essay, pp. 102–106. ED.]

[9] *An Essay on the Principle of Population*, 6th edn., 1826, Ward, Lock, London, Book IV, Chapter X, pp. 501–502.

† [The terms 'giver' and 'taker' will be used as more homely alternatives to the legal 'donor' and 'donee' and the fiscal/social service 'beneficiary' or 'recipient'.—ED.]

[10] What follows is a simplified version of a more technical analysis in my 'Some Fundamental Economics of the Charity Market', in David B. Johnson and Thomas R. Ireland, *The Economics of Charity*, ed. Gordon Tullock, Public Choice Society, Blacksburg, Virginia, 1970, pp. 94–102.

basis for starting our analysis. We must distinguish between two general categories of welfare:

(1) general welfare in which the giver (Able) desires an increase in the total welfare of the taker (Baker); or

(2) specific welfare in which the giver prefers the taker to increase his consumption of a specific commodity.

This dichtomy has important policy implications when injected into the debate between those who favour expenditure to aid the poor and those who favour income or wealth distribution. The important question is: Do taxpayers-citizens prefer directly to alleviate the general level of poverty, or do they want the poor to increase the consumption of *specific* goods such as education, medical care, food, or clothing?

Even if we know that Able obtains satisfaction from Baker's consumption of a specific good, say fish, we cannot be sure that Able will act on this preference because he may value an increase in his own consumption of fish more than he values an increase in Baker's consumption. The relevant consideration is not whether the individual is absolutely selfish or absolutely altruistic but whether, at the margin, he prefers an increase in his neighbour's consumption more than an increase in his own.

If Able does have a *relevant* preference for Baker's fish consumption, he could give the fish to Baker (i.e. at a zero price). But this course would be inefficient. Because Able wants only to increase Baker's fish consumption, he can accomplish this objective by lowering the price. As the price is lowered, Baker will buy more fish. Also, if Able can charge a positive but lower-than-market price for the fish, he will provide more fish to Baker than he would if he were unable to ask a positive price.

The policy implications of this simple statement are numerous and important. First, many individuals believe that charity occurs only at a zero transfer price. Titmuss, for example, believed that individuals engage in charity (the 'gift relationship') only when-they donate blood at a zero price. This is incorrect. Individuals may accept a positive price when they are acting charitably, whereas they would demand a *higher* price if they were acting as economic men. Second, when the giver is able to charge a positive but lower-than-market price for the transfer good, the quantity of goods transferred is larger than when the giver is unable to exact a price from the taker. Third, charitable preferences will introduce price divergences in the market. Assume that Able and Baker can buy, but not sell, fish on the world market. Able will adjust his purchases of fish to the world price but Baker will adjust his purchases, at least at the margin, to the lower price being offered to him by Able. Economists view price divergences with disfavour because they have established that consumer welfare would be increased if all consumers adjusted their purchases to the same price. Some economists and policy-makers argue that the existence of price divergences constitutes anti-competitive behaviour, and in the US the firms so engaged are subject to anti-trust prosecution. It is, therefore, important to note that if specific welfare is introduced, price divergences must exist if efficiency is to be achieved.

The previous discussion ignored time. When time is introduced Baker will become aware of Able's preferences and he will alter his behaviour. Hence, Baker will consume less fish in order to induce Able to provide more at a lower price. Once the taker knows that the giver is 'concerned' that he should consume a specified good, say education or medical care, the taker may reduce his consumption of that good, and rely on the giver to provide the additional amount. In effect, then, the giver is merely substituting his provision of the good for the amount previously provided by the taker. The giver has not accomplished his objective of increasing the taker's consumption of the specific good because the taker may now use the money saved on the charity good to purchase other goods. This strategic behaviour on the part of the taker has resulted in the giver's preference of specific welfare being converted into general welfare by the taker. This is a serious problem for charitable provision, whether through the charity or political markets. It is a problem many of its advocates completely ignore.[11]

In the previous analysis, we assumed that Baker could not resell his fish; if he could, he could obtain fish below the market price from Able and resell it at the market price. Baker's income (general welfare) would be increased, but the objective of the giver (specific welfare) would not be achieved. For example, despite the precautionary measures taken on food stamps issued to the poor in the US, the poor often sold their food stamps to non-recipients and used the money for unqualified purposes.

---

[11] If Able knows that Baker is artificially reducing his purchases of fish to induce Able to provide more, Able may attempt to conceal his welfare preferences, thus making it difficult for observers (i.e. social scientists) to determine whether Able is indeed acting charitably or not.

The welfare economics of charitable behaviour

What can be gleaned from this simplified analysis?

(1) Economic analysis can be applied to the choice behaviour of charitable man as well as economic man.

(2) The dichotomy between general and specific welfare can be injected into the debate between people who favour specific expenditures to aid the poor and those who favour income or wealth redistribution. While one plan produces price distortions and the other does not, their relative efficiency cannot be evaluated until the preferences of the givers, in this case the taxpayers/citizens, are examined.

(3) Price divergences, which have rightly been anathematised by economists, are required in some circumstances to internalise the specific welfare-charity preferences of individuals.

(4) Givers may be unable to achieve their goal of specific welfare if takers can re-arrange the commodity mix of their market basket. The 'increased' provision by the giver may merely reduce the taker's purchases.

(5) Givers may be unable to achieve specific welfare if takers are able to resell the charitable good on the market.

(6) There are welfare transfers in the private market. In its day-to-day operations, it redistributes wealth from those who misuse their resources to those who use them wisely. It redistributes wealth to those who own resources (including human resources) which produce goods and services that satisfy new consumer demands and technology and away from those who own resources no longer in demand. And in its efficient allocation of goods and resources it provides for a degree of relative redistribution. The automobile by increasing the mobility of the poor, the clothing industry by providing the poor man with inexpensive synthetics, the radio and TV industries by providing inexpensive communications, have probably altered the relative distribution of income more than any foundation or social programme.

These distributions are well known and are part-and-parcel of the *homo economicus* private market. Beyond this, however, the private market permits the '*homo altruisticus*' redistribution of wealth. It permits individual givers to redistribute wealth by selling commodities below the market price.

The existence of a positive price for a commodity (blood, food, housing) does not mean that the supplier is devoid of altruistic motives. If the supplier has a preference for the buyer to consume units of the commodity he is selling, he can express this preference by lowering the price. Indeed, if the seller were able to express his altruistic motivations only by offering his goods at a zero price, the quantity he would supply would be much less, perhaps even zero.

In the real world, some individuals and firms provide transfers in money or kind by selling lower and buying higher than the market price. Recently, firms in the US have been hiring members of minority groups and training them when more experienced and better-qualified majorities were available at the same wage-rate. Another good example is the store owner who, after some local natural disaster, does not raise his prices but continues to sell his goods below the prices obtainable in the market-place.[12] The housewife who buys Girl Guide biscuits at a price higher than her neighbourhood grocer's is expressing an altruistic motivation. Of course, many private market transfers are intertwined with the charity and political markets. Store owners may not raise their prices or firms may hire minorities because of social or political pressures.[13]

Whatever their motivation, however, it is not clear that such actions are desirable from the viewpoint of the rest of the community. The firms which hire unqualified minorities produce products of lower quality, higher prices, lower dividends, or some combination of them, and discriminate against the more qualified non-minorities. The store owner who refuses to use the price system as a discriminatory mechanism must use some other form of discrimination, such as queues, relatives, beauty, race, religion, past patronage, etc., which are not very efficient and may not be morally acceptable ways of ensuring that those who most want the products get them. The queuing system does permit the 'queuer' to express some intensity of preference by his willingness and ability to stand in line. But in its simple form queuing may become a particularly dangerous system. First, it rewards those who are non-productive and whose opportunity cost of time is relatively low. Second, it is

[12] Interesting examples and good economic analysis applied to this unexplored subject are in Douglas C. Daly and Howard Kunreuther, *The Economics of National Disasters*, The Free Press, New York, 1969.

[13] On the basis of the analysis presented below, it is suggested that it is the large, very 'visible' firms which are most subject to both social and political pressures to hold prices down and to hire minority groups.

most difficult for sellers and government agencies to devise feasible and effective ways of prohibiting resale in the grey and black markets, which are less effective than the open pricing system. Third, the relatively low price received by the seller does not enable or induce him to increase the rate at which new supplies of the commodity will flow into the area. While welfare transfers can be accomplished through the private market, it is not clear that they are indeed charitable for most of the citizens.

The increase, if any, in Baker's fish consumption in this simple two-man model is both a private and a public good. It is a public good in the sense that both Able and Baker obtain benefits from Baker's consumption; but in another and very important sense, the amount of welfare fish consumed by Baker is a private good because there is a direct relationship between the amount provided by the individual giver and the total amount of welfare fish received by Baker. The *social* problems of charity associated with large numbers of individuals do not exist in this model.

B. Charity in a Large-numbered Community

In a two-person world there are no social problems because the two individuals can satisfy their preferences through charity, force, or trade involving only them. There are no third parties with which to enter intrigues, each is reasonably aware of the other's preferences and actions, and the giver knows that only he can increase the welfare of his fellow citizen. In the simple model above, Able was confronted with the strategic behaviour of Baker, but he did not have to worry about the strategic behaviour of other citizens.

Once we assume that Able is joined by a thousand other individuals similarly concerned about Baker's consumption of fish, the problems increase many-fold. In particular, the amount of 'welfare' fish that Baker receives is not in a one-to-one relationship with the amount provided by Able. Baker's fish consumption, at least at the margin, now becomes a public good. Able will benefit if others provide fish to Baker and they will benefit if he gives fish to Baker. His enjoyment of knowing that Baker's welfare has increased does not decrease the amount of pleasure that the other individuals can experience. Hence, Baker's consumption of fish qualifies as a public good, not because Able as well as Baker obtains benefits from such consumption, but because Able and the thousand other 'givers' obtain benefits from Baker's consumption of fish.

The non-collective charitable provision of public goods embodies a paradox. If each of the thousand individuals, acting in ignorance of the knowledge that other individuals were acting similarly, contributed fish to Baker (or sold fish below the market price), the amount of specific welfare extended to Baker would be over-extended. If each individual gives a street beggar a penny because he values the increase in the beggar's welfare more than he values the penny, the total amount of welfare extended to the beggar will be much more than each individual would want it to be if he knew that other citizens made the same decision. If each individual acts as a classic 'free rider' and does not give the beggar a penny because he believes that others will, the amount of welfare will be under-extended. The quantity of the public good, therefore, will be over- or under-extended depending upon the individual's knowledge of the existence, potential or real, of other contributors.

Purely individual contributions in a society of large numbers are not likely to provide the optimum quantity of welfare or of any other public good. Hence, if the welfare of Baker is the objective, this analysis suggests that it be collectivised. The conclusion reached by most political economists is that such collectivisation must be achieved through the *political* market, in which the 'free-rider' problem is avoided through the selective use of taxation and imprisonment. Casual reference to the real world, however, suggests the possibility that such collectivisation may be achieved through a collective but *private* intermediary in the charity market.

The economics of private intermediation

An analysis of intermediation in the charity market is subject to many difficulties. First, little research has been done, and second, it is difficult for economists to conceive of charitable actions as constituting a market. There are so many individual motivations and objectives and so many varying levels of conscious action that it is extremely difficult to develop a methodology which will aid in understanding the complex inter-relationships in this market. The following is presented as a preliminary analysis.

(1) *Motivations for contributions*

The amount of welfare or other type of good (national defence, education, medical care, housing, blood, etc.) that individuals prefer to provide to other individuals is a matter of taste and is not readily amenable to scientific analysis, but the institutions through which preferences are revealed and decisions are made can be analysed.

The relevant question is: What negative or positive inducements will avoid the large-number and 'free-rider' problems? Although there are many sub-categories, the three most salient classes are:

(a) *The religious motive.* This motive has had a tremendous historical importance, and, while diminishing slightly in recent years, it must still be listed as a major motivation.

Slightly less than one-half of all charitable contributions in the US are channelled through religious organisations. Most religions influence the tastes of the individual by teaching him to 'give what thou hast to the poor', 'treat thy neighbour as thyself', etc., and by providing a selective incentive for the individual to contribute. As an analytical purist might put it: 'There is no free ride to heaven', or, as Aldous Huxley once noted: 'Charity is a peculiar species of fire insurance'.[14] Religious societies also are so organised that in small number groups, the problems of large numbers can be avoided and contributions can be obtained more effectively. Hence, it is difficult to separate the religious motive from the income and social-pressure motives.

(b) *The income motive.* Individuals may be charitable to increase their income stream, to improve working conditions, to obtain political office, etc.[15] A charity 'tax' schedule may be established or adopted by an employer which determines the 'fair share' to be contributed by each employee. If the individual does not donate approximately this amount, he may believe that his income stream, widely defined, will be adversely affected. Generally, this income motive can be expected to be more prevalent among firms or unions that possess a degree of monopoly/monopsony power.[16]

---

[14] Or as Bishop Fulton Sheen said: 'This giving [to Catholic Charities] is not giving up anything but exchanging temporal wealth for spiritual wealth. The Catholics of New York City are not asked to give up $2,500,000. Catholic Charities has no drive: it is conducting an exchange'.

[15] Many political leaders in the US, particularly local and state, start their political careers by working for and contributing towards charitable activities. This motive may be listed separately, but it is analytically very close to both the income and the social-pressure motives.

[16] Since this 'required' giving reduces the real wage of the individual worker, it would not be expected in industries in which there are competitive resources or product markets. I attempted to correlate concentration ratios with data on per-employee contributions by industry, but the data were not consistent with Standard US Classifications and could not be honestly adjusted without losing much of the 'truth'. Casual observation of the data, however, suggests that employees in 'visible', i.e. locally or nationally prominent, and non-competitive industries contributed more per person than the employees in non-visible and competitive industries. Visible firms may also be more amenable to community pressures and thus more likely to adopt a 'fair-share' plan for their em-

(c) *Psychic benefits as Kantian acts.* In *The Gift Relationship* Professor Titmuss seemed to place considerable importance on the existence of the volunteer community giver who, according to him, is the source of all blood in Britain. These givers are supposedly engaged in a completely unselfish act because they obtain psychic benefits from the mere act of giving blood. Professor Thomas Ireland has called this desire to perform a 'good 'act, as distinguished from the real purposes or accomplishment of the act, the 'Kantian' motive, named after the German philosopher Immanuel Kant, who argued that 'goodness' requires complete separation from personal gain of the individual decision-maker.[17]

The Kantian motive is not very important in a simple community where Able gives fish to Baker because he can observe the consequence of his preferences, i.e. Baker's increased fish consumption. In a larger community this direct one-to-one relationship is not possible, and the 'free-rider' problem becomes important. If an individual wishes one or more other individuals to consume additional units of a commodity, he is unaware of the preferences and actions of his fellow citizens and the effects of their actions upon the total provision of the good to the taker. A related problem occurs when there is a relatively large number of potential takers. No single potential giver is able to affect the welfare level of all potential takers. Therefore, some selective incentive is necessary to induce the individual to contribute. One of these selective incentives is the 'good feeling' the individual receives from the *act* of contributing (Kantian motive), not to be confused with the *benefits* he obtains from accomplishing the act.

Undoubtedly, many individuals contribute blood, money, time, and commodities for this reason, Determining motivations, however, is not easy, especially if individuals act as if they enjoy contributing toward some worthy cause but, in truth, do so because of subtle but real pressures placed on them by their neighbours, friends, fellow workers, etc. An apparent Kantian may be far removed from a real Kantian and, even if the individual were a real Kantian, it is

---

ployees. (David B. Johnson, 'Fundamental Economics of the Charity Market', University of Virginia, also available from University Microfilm, Ann Arbor, Michigan: pp. 178–198 discuss charity taxes, their incidence and 'double taxation', and pp. 221–224 list United Fund contributions per employee and per firm by industry classification.)

[17] 'Charity Budgeting', in *The Economics of Charity*, *op. cit.*, pp. 22–26. A revised version of Professor Ireland's original treatise is reproduced in Part I of this *Readings* as Essay No. 4.

not clear that society could depend on this motive day-in, day-out, through the tedious motions of time, to generate sufficient support for such necessary activities as education, medical research, and provision of blood whether or not such contributions elicit personal good feelings or happen to be in vogue.

Analysing the effects of Kantian-motivated social organisation requires much study and research, but at the present stage of analytical development not much, apart from stating the equilibrium conditions, can be said about it.

(d) *Social pressures*. Social pressures may account for a considerable number of philanthropic acts. Such a statement should be interpreted neither as a cynicism nor as criticism of philanthropists. A society in which individuals do good deeds to win the approval of their fellows cannot be adjudged to be undesirable, nor can the well-publicised patron or patroness of the arts be accused of performing useless functions.

Adam Smith's invisible hand, the rationale of which is that individuals best serve their fellow man by pursuing their self-interests, might be a much more general and therefore a more useful theory than he, or his most ardent followers, realised. Men do not change moral gears as they shift from one type of market activity (private) to another (political or charity); they merely maximise (optimise) different values or goals.

The invisible hand is altered but not negated if individuals optimise social approval instead of profits. We have much to learn about channelling and directing such energies; the most serious obstacle is the lack of a *Wealth of Nations** describing the mechanism of the invisible, or perhaps visible, hand in the political and charity markets. By positing social pressure (or its inverse, social approval) as the motivating agent in the charity market, we might be able to say something, however weak and tenuous in the initial stages of the analysis, about the choice mechanism in the charity market and the resulting provision and allocation of resources.

We can begin with the hypothesis that an individual who refuses to contribute towards a well-recognised and approved public good is likely to incur social disapproval or social pressure. Assume that a charity agency wishes to collect and distribute contributions for a

* [An absorbing study of the genesis of *The Wealth of Nations* and the concept of the 'invisible hand' is in the biography of Adam Smith by E. G. West, *Adam Smith: The Man and His Works*, Arlington House, New Rochelle, N.Y., 1969.—ED.]

generally accepted public good,[18] and that it skilfully applies social pressure to the potential 'free rider' who may have a preference for the public good but realises that his contribution will have no perceptible effect on the total provision and that he cannot be excluded from its benefits.

How does social pressure affect the individual as additional units are applied to him? Although he can be expected to place a cost on each additional derisive remark or social disapproval, the marginal cost or disutility he incurs per unit of social pressure will decrease as additional units of social pressure are applied to him. Assuming that all individuals are thoroughly and equally acquainted with the potential 'free rider', as the size of the community is increased, the total social pressure experienced by the individual increases, though at a decreasing rate.

As population is increased it is unrealistic to assume that all individuals remain thoroughly familiar with the potential 'free rider'. The probability that any individual is aware of the actions of any other individual decreases as population increases owing to the larger physical permutations, the compartmentalisation of the individual's life, etc. Hence, if the costs of social pressures increase at a decreasing rate as the size of the community increases and if, beyond some point, the likelihood that all individuals are acquainted with one another decreases as population increases, the net result is that the effective amount of social pressure which can be applied to each individual decreases as the size of the community increases.

The individual living in a small community who attempts a free ride on the charitable contributions of others will be confronted with higher social pressures than one living in a large community. Thus, the *per capita* contributions of small community residents can be expected to be larger (assuming equal incomes) than large city residents and, therefore, small communities can be expected to finance a relatively larger number of public goods through the charity market than large communities. For example, in many small American communities fire protection and ambulance services are provided through the charity market, whereas in large communities they are provided through the political markets.

Why welfare services have been politicised

The social-pressure thesis offers a plausible explanation of the

[18] A theory of a charity fund would require a rather lengthy and technical discussion. We assume that the agency exists and its goal is to maximise contributions.

historical phenomenon that many public goods (education, welfare) initially provided through the charity market were shifted to the political market as their relative quantities expanded and individuals' cost-shares became larger than the amount of social pressure which could be applied to them. Increasing urbanisation reinforced this trend because it reduced the effective amount of social pressure which could be applied to the individual.

This framework also enables us to analyse the *macro*-feasibility of the charity market and the *micro*-actions of fund-raising agencies. One way for the fund-maximising charity agency to increase contributions is to increase social pressure through advertising which projects the objective as worthy and to encourage individuals to act as though they were pure Kantians. Charity agencies not only inform the public through such advertisements but they nourish the idea that the eradication of disease X, the elimination of hunger among the Whobians, and a full shelf of blood in every hospital are desirable community goals; and, most important for our purposes, these advertisements result in the application of increased pressures to the 'free rider'.

A second strategy is to sub-divide large communities into smaller decision-making groups in which the societal costs are larger. Although it is seldom possible to re-create the inter-personal relationships of small communities, segmenting large communities into employment and neighbourhood groups, unions, clubs, lodges, etc., and assigning quotas to these sub-groups, permits social pressures to be applied more effectively.[19]

[19] University alumni fund-raising techniques might be an example. The committee would be expected to promote an advertising campaign pointing out the benefits accruing to alumni and to the community from a better-endowed university. The campaign committee might even sponsor dinners or parties in various communities for the announced purpose of enabling the alumni to become re-acquainted. These activities contribute to an upward shifting of social pressure because the individual alumni members, now that they are aware of the public-good aspects of the campaign and are more familiar with each other, will face stronger social pressures if they refuse to contribute. When the fund-raising campaign begins, the total alumni community would be segmented into localities, class years, former fraternity affiliations, etc., and an alumnus acquainted with many potential donors appointed as chairman or group captain. The names of the donors and the amount they contribute would, of course, be published in the next issue of the alumni magazine. These expectations were developed not from empirical observations but from the conclusions of the social-pressure theory. (The reader can test this theory by applying these conclusions to his experiences with university or other fund-raising campaigns.)

A casual investigation of instructions given to fund-raising campaign leaders for the United Fund and the Red Cross in the US also verifies the theory. The instructions encourage the leaders to divide the residential community into sections and to recruit

(2) *Summary*

Once we move beyond a simple two-person model of charity and introduce numerous potential givers and takers, the amount of transfers could be more or less than optimal unless collective provision is made. One form of collectivisation is the political mechanism, another the charity market. Provision of transfers through the political market entails the selective cost of monetary fines and imprisonment for the taxpayer-citizen who attempts a 'free ride'. If the public goods are to be provided through the charity market, there must again be a selective incentive. Although various selective incentives exist in the charity market, including the Kantian motive, the social-pressure theory is useful in describing a segment of individual and institutional behaviour in the charity market. If social pressures which can be applied to the free-riding individual are inversely related to population, the ratio of public goods provided through the charity market would be expected to be higher in smaller and lower in larger communities. Over time, increased urbanisation (individuals are living in larger communities in which social pressure is less effective) would diminish the relative importance of the charity market. But this is a *ceteris paribus* argument, and other variables do not remain constant. Charity agencies attempt to increase the amount of social presure through advertising, and they modify the large-number problem through their solicitation techniques.

III. WHICH MARKET?

There are at least three market mechanisms through which individuals may produce and allocate goods: private, political and charity. Private goods and personal charity (both specific and general) can be produced and allocated efficiently through the private market. Collective or public goods can be provided through the political or charity markets. Because relatively little is known about the choice mechanisms of these two markets, especially those of the charity market, it is difficult to compare the relative efficiency of each in the provision of public goods. A brief discussion of decision-making,

workers from each section to solicit in their neighbourhood. The leaders are instructed to organise solicitations in clubs, churches, parent-teacher organisations, business firms, etc. United Fund guide-lines state: 'larger contributions are to be solicited by two or three . . . personal, business, or club acquaintances'. It appears there is some empirical content to the social-pressure theory.

external and inclusion costs might provide some helpful generalisations.[20]

Relative efficiency of the market mechanisms

Decision-making costs

Decision-making costs are those arising from the time and effort expended by the individual in attempting to secure an acceptable agreement from other individuals. These costs rise as the number of individuals required to approve a plan or decision increases. Decision-making costs are applicable in both the political and charity markets, but they are likely to be lower in the charity market. First, since most individuals do not participate directly or indirectly in the decision-making process in the collective charity market, their decision-making costs are lower. Secondly, the 'public' goods provided through the charity market may be 'public' only to groups of individuals who can voluntarily provide them through a small agency or committee in which the fewer number of individuals necessary to reach a decision results in lower decision-making costs.

External costs

External costs are those which the individual expects to have imposed on him by the adverse action (votes) of his fellow citizens. Given a decision-making rule of less than unanimity, there is always a probability that others will make decisions the individual would not select. An individual who places a low or negative value upon education (defence, welfare services, etc.), but is required to pay taxes to support education, etc., suffers negative external costs in the political market. Similarly, 'wrong' decisions may be made in the charitable market which the individual is induced to support because of the threat of social pressures. Charitable contributions to private (or public) colleges induced by social pressures in the charity market constitute an external cost to the individual, the same as tax payments to support public colleges. Hence, the theoretical concepts are identical in the two markets, but the varying structures and cost levels in each market merit more discussion.

If an individual strongly dislikes the decisions of his fellow citizens (or their representatives) in the political market, he may refuse to

---

20 The terms 'decision-making' and 'external costs' were originally introduced by Professors James M. Buchanan and Gordon Tullock in describing costs in the political market: *The Calculus of Consent: Logical Foundations of Constitutional Democracy*, University of Michigan Press, Ann Arbor, 1962.

pay taxes and go to prison. Since this is (for most!) a high-cost alternative, it is not expected to be, and seldom is, selected. If the individual dislikes a decision made in the charity market, his alternative is to suffer social pressure. Since the cost of 'opting out' is lower in the charity market than in the political market, the individual is confronted with lower expected external costs. Hence, the individual who places a high value on minimising external costs would select the charity market, However, he will expect to be in the majority on some issues, and he knows that in the charity market the minority might fail to contribute to the provision of a public good because they can select the relatively low-cost alternative of social pressure. If the good were provided through the political market, the certainty of provision would be much stronger. Hence, the individual must weigh the value he places on his freedom to opt out of an action he does not desire against the value he places on the certainty of provision of public goods he does.

Inclusion costs

A third type of cost which has not been considered by political-market analysts is the cost to some individuals of extending the voting franchise to other individuals; the author prefers to call these 'inclusion' costs. The decision-making framework in the US and some other countries is so structured that one level of decision-making—the constitutional—determines the broad class of activities to be decided upon through political action, while the other level—the operational—decides the quantities, revenues, and expenditures for goods on which the constitution permits political action. If a higher ratio of affirmative votes is necessary at the constitutional than at the operational decision level, inclusion costs may be significant for a relative comparison of the political and charity markets.

Assume a community composed of 50 rich people (R's) and 60 poor people (P's), with the R's possessing the voting franchise, and assume that a constitutional amendment must be approved by 75 per cent of the electorate while operational decisions require only 50 per cent. Assume all R's have a preference for transferring some amount of income to the P's. The R's may now vote for a constitutional amendment permitting welfare transfers to the P's and can proceed to vote for operational bills in which they tax themselves to provide welfare transfers to the P's. So long as the P's remain disenfranchised, the R's will be able to provide through the political market what, from their point of view, is an optimal level of welfare.

If, however, the P's have the franchise in addition to the R's, the R's will not be willing to vote for the constitutional amendment permitting welfare transfers because they know that at the operational level of decision-making they will be in the minority and the P's will vote for a non-optimal (as viewed by the R's) extension of welfare. Hence, even if the R's prefer a moderate amount of welfare transfers to the P's, they will refuse to vote for constitutional approval of such transfers through the political market because of the majority position at the operational level of the P's, whom the R's fear will vote for radical redistribution.

The charity market presents an alternative mechanism through which the R's can provide for optimal transfers while avoiding the inclusion costs of a political market with universal suffrage. The charity market permits the R's to form voluntary groups to provide moderate transfers while, at the same time, excluding the P's from the decision-making process. Hence, one would expect the charity market to be relatively large where the political franchise is widely extended and exercised and where the constitution is relevant, whereas in communities where the franchise is not widely used the provision of welfare through the political market may be relatively larger. Obviously, if the voting franchise is extended within a given constitution or if the constitution is amended by judicial processes or simple majority voting, this conclusion would be invalid.

IV. CONCLUSION

The charity market is an alternative to the political market in the provision of public goods. Which market is more efficient in such provision is difficult to determine. According to the theory developed in this essay the feasibility of charitable provision is affected by the size and stability of social and neighbourhood organisations and the adeptness of intermediaries in developing solicitation techniques and methods of applying social pressure. Increasing urbanisation and a weakening of the social and fraternal fabric within community and service organisations suggest that the charity market will be losing ground. On the other hand, the increasing sophistication of the intermediaries, especially in their use of occupational groups to solicit contributions and to apply social pressure, may offset this trend.

In evaluating these two markets some of the variables that must be included are decision-making, external and inclusion costs. Decision-making costs clearly favour the charity market in the provision of goods which are 'public' to a relatively small number of individuals. Neighbourhood beautification committees, hobby organisations, industry trade associations, etc., are examples of groups providing such goods. External costs cut both ways depending upon the weights assigned to individual freedom and to certainty of provision. Inclusion costs inject voting systems into the analysis and suggest that potential donors may not agree to a constitution permitting welfare payments through the political market if the voting franchise is widely extended.

Appendix
Statistics on American Charity

TABLE 1.—CONTRIBUTIONS, BY SOURCE: SELECTED YEARS, 1960 TO 1971

(Billions of Dollars and Percentages of Total)

		1960	1965	1970	1971
Bequests	$	0·62	1·02	2·20	3·00
	%	*6·9*	*8·4*	*11·3*	*14·2*
Corporations	$	0·48	0·79	1·00	1·00
	%	*5·4*	*6·4*	*5·1*	*4·7*
Foundations	$	0·66	1·13	1·90	2·05
	%	*7·5*	*9·4*	*9·7*	*9·7*
Individuals	$	7·15	9·23	14·40	15·10
	%	*80·2*	*75·8*	*73·9*	*71·4*
Total	$	8·91	12·17	19·50	21·15
	%	*100·0*	*100·0*	*100·0*	*100·0*

Source: *Giving, U.S.A.*, American Association of Fund Raising Counsel, Inc., 1971, 1972. Percentages computed by author.

TABLE 2.—CORPORATE CONTRIBUTIONS: ABSOLUTE AMOUNTS AND PERCENTAGE OF CORPORATE PRE-TAX NET INCOME, SELECTED YEARS, 1950 TO 1970

Year	Amounts (millions of $)	% of Net Pre-Tax Income
1950	252	0·59
1955	415	0·85
1960	482	0·97
1965	785	1·01
1970	990*	1·31*

Sources: Council for Financial Aid to Education; Internal Revenue Service.

*Estimates

TABLE 3.—ALLOCATION OF CORPORATE CONTRIBUTIONS:[1] SELECTED YEARS, 1959 TO 1970

	Percentages of Total		
	1959	1965	1970
Health and welfare	45·1	41·5	38·6
Education	39·1	38·4	37·6
Culture (cultural centres, performing arts, museums, etc.)[2]	2·9 (Culture and Civic causes combined)	2·8	5·3
Civic causes (municipal and community improvement, good government, and the like)[2]		5·8	8·1
Other	12·9	11·5	10·3
Total	100·0	100·0	100·0

Source: The Conference Board, *Biennial Survey of Company Contributions*, 1972.

TABLE 4.—ALLOCATION OF PRIVATE CHARITABLE CONTRIBUTIONS: SELECTED YEARS, 1960 TO 1971

(Billions of Dollars and Percentages of Total)

		1960	1965	1970	1971
Religion	$	4·55	5·98	8·30	8·60
	%	*51·0*	*48·9*	*42·5*	*40·7*
Education	$	1·43	2·08	3·10	3·30
	%	*16·0*	*17·1*	*15·9*	*15·6*
Social	$	1·34	0·86	1·40	1·55
Welfare	%	*15·0*	*7·0*	*7·2*	*7·3*
Health	$	1·07	2·08	3·20	3·40
	%	*12·0*	*17·1*	*16·4*	*16·1*
Miscellaneous	$	0·53	1·22	3·50	4·30
	%	*6·0*	*10·0*	*18·0*	*20·3*
Total	$	8·92	12·22	19·50	21·15
	%	*100·0*	*100·0*	*100·0*	*100·0*

Source: American Association of Fund Raising Counsel, Inc.

---

[1] Data based on results of survey of 401 companies in 1970, 540 companies in 1965, and 280 companies in 1959.

[2] Culture and civic causes were not tabulated separately prior to 1965.

TABLE 5.—CURRENT REVENUE SOURCES OF INSTITUTIONS OF HIGHER LEARNING: SELECTED YEARS, 1950 TO 1969

(Millions of Dollars and Percentages of Total)

	1950 %	1960 %	1969 %
Student Fees	16·6	20·0	20·2
Endowment Earnings	4·0	3·6	2·1
Federal, State and Local Government	45·4	44·3	42·1
Private Gifts and Grants	5·0	6·6	3·2
Organised Activities Related to Instruction	4·7	4·2	2·9
Miscellaneous	1·5	2·3	5·4
Auxiliary Enterprises and Activities	22·8	18·9	24·1
Total Income	100·0	100·0	100·0
	($2,376)	($5,786)	($18,875)

Source: US Department of Health, Education, and Welfare, Office of Education.

TABLE 6.—CORPORATE CONTRIBUTIONS TO EDUCATION AS PERCENTAGE OF CORPORATE PRE-TAX INCOME: SELECTED YEARS, 1950 TO 1970

Year	% of Pre-tax net income
1950	0·10
1955	0·21
1960	0·36
1965	0·36
1970	0·45

Sources: Internal Revenue Service; US Department of Commerce; Council for Financial Aid to Education.

TABLE 7.—CONTRIBUTIONS AS PERCENTAGE OF ADJUSTED GROSS INCOME BY ADJUSTED GROSS INCOME CLASSES, 1970

Adjusted Gross Income Groups $	Adjusted Gross Income $ (000's)	Contributions as % of AGI	Weighted Marginal Tax Rate	Adjusted Contributions (after tax savings) as % of AGI
1,000 Under 2,000	103,556	6·0	16·46	5·0
2,000 Under 3,000	1,051,948	5·4	18·54	4·4
3,000 Under 4,000	4,141,188	4·9	18·31	4·0
4,000 Under 5,000	7,871,096	4·1	20·55	3·2
5,000 Under 6,000	10,636,643	3·8	20·29	3·0
6,000 Under 7,000	13,868,644	3·1	21·10	2·5
7,000 Under 8,000	17,020,410	3·0	20·67	2·4
8,000 Under 9,000	21,315,103	2·9	23·21	2·2
9,000 Under 10,000	24,441,835	2·8	22·93	2·1
10,000 Under 11,000	26,037,522	2·7	22·85	2·1
11,000 Under 12,000	26,979,503	2·5	22·85	1·9
12,000 Under 13,000	26,473,844	2·4	25·95	1·8
13,000 Under 14,000	25,935,759	2·4	25·95	1·8
14,000 Under 15,000	24,341,288	2·4	26·19	1·8
15,000 Under 20,000	84,001,581	2·4	28·15	1·7
20,000 Under 25,000	39,428,715	2·5	33·61	1·7

TABLE 7.—CONTRIBUTIONS AS PERCENTAGE OF ADJUSTED GROSS INCOME BY ADJUSTED GROSS INCOME CLASSES, 1970—*continued*

Adjusted Gross Income Groups $	Adjusted Gross Income $ (000's)	Contri-butions as % of AGI	Weighted Marginal Tax Rate	Adjusted Contri-butions (after tax savings) as % of AGI
25,000 Under 30,000	19,797,009	2·5	38·08	1·6
30,000 Under 50,000	32,926,822	2·7	46·62	1·4
50,000 Under 100,000	22,703,663	3·3	56·85	1·4
100,000 +	14,140,284	7·3	67·56	2·4

Source: Preliminary data on contributions and adjusted gross income provided to the author by US Treasury; data published in *Statistics of Income, 1970*.

PART II
Application: Blood

1. The Economics of Giving and Selling Blood

M. H. COOPER

Reader in Social Economics, University of Exeter

and

A. J. CULYER

Assistant Director, Institute of Social and Economic Research, University of York

THE AUTHORS

MICHAEL H. COOPER graduated from the University of Leicester in 1961. He has taught economics at the Universities of Keele, Stanford and Exeter where he is at present Reader in Social Economics. He is Editor of the journal *Social and Economic Administration* and of a series of occasional papers in the same field.

His publications include *Prices and Profits in the Pharmaceutical Industry* (Pergamon Press, Oxford, 1966); with A. J. Culyer, *The Price of Blood* (Hobart Paper 41, Institute of Economic Affairs, London, 1968), *Health Economics* (Penguin Readings in Economics, London, 1973), *The Pharmaceutical Industry in the United Kingdom* (Economists Advisory Group and Dun and Bradstreet, London, 1973); with A. K. Maynard, *The Price of Air Travel* (Hobart Paper 53, Institute of Economic Affairs, London, 1971); with A. J. Cooper, *International Price Comparison* (National Economic Development Office, London, 1972); and numerous papers on social and industrial economics in collections of essays and academic journals.

ANTHONY J. CULYER (See Part I, Essay 3, p. 34).

I. INTRODUCTION

Are moral considerations so important as to outweigh the implications for policy derived from economic analysis? Is giving intrinsically preferable to selling? If so, what role can selling have in a society claiming to be civilised, humane and just? Are the undoubted imperfections of the American blood market solely, or even mainly, attributable to a commercial sector? Would the same imperfections inevitably follow payment for blood in the British Isles? In this essay we attempt to respond to these challenges and extend our earlier analysis by considering the economics of giving.

Characteristically, economic analysis has proceeded on the simplifying assumption that most human beings are primarily motivated outside their families by more or less selfish considerations. There is vast evidence that the amount of resources people are in practice prepared to make available for the use of others is extremely small.[1] Even massive calamities in far away places such as those recently in Bangladesh, India and West Africa meet with a response that is typically mean as a proportion of his resources the average person is prepared to sacrifice, though equally typically total subscriptions tend to be accompanied by substantial self-congratulation. Within his community the average individual is likely to be a little more generous, though even the large quantity of resources distributed through the 'Welfare State' goes mostly to persons who are in no sense poor, while those who are have to get along on miserly 'gifts' from the community at large.[2] These expenditures possibly exaggerate the real generosity of spirit in the community as a whole, for the poor too have a vote and may vote (selfishly) for assistance for themselves.[3] Alternatively, the envious rich may vote for aid to the poor so that the even richer have some of their wealth taxed away.

A more general approach

The characteristic assumption of self first and foremost seems therefore a good approximation to reality. Nevertheless, it is not a *perfect*

[1] This is to infer people's motives from what they *do*. What they *say* indicates a completely opposite assessment of their attitudes. We assume it is behaviour that is being analysed.

[2] Thomas R. Ireland and David B. Johnson indicate some measures of the strength of individuals' desires to give in a context of social policy in Gordon Tullock (ed.), *The Economics of Charity*, Center for Study of Public Choice, Blacksburg, Virginia, 1970.

[3] Conversely, the Pakistanis in what was East Pakistan and India had no vote in Britain.

description and in studying human behaviour that is evidently more or less altruistic it becomes necessary to remove it. Fortunately, there is nothing in economic analysis that compels us to retain the assumption of selfishness; so it is possible to study an 'economics of giving' as well as an 'economics of selling'.

The most general approach would be to assume that individuals are neither entirely selfish nor entirely altruistic. This is the one we adopt. We shall concentrate on applying the theory to blood supply with its special technological and ethical aspects. This fuller analysis corroborates the conclusions in our *Hobart Paper*,[4] but we shall also derive a wider range of implications outside the National Health Service (NHS). First we reply to some of the criticisms made of our earlier argument.

II. THE SHORTAGE OF BLOOD

With the advance of medical knowledge, human blood has over the past 30 years become an essential therapeutic and life-saving agent in rapidly-growing demand. World-wide shortages have emerged and countries have sought various solutions to maintaining supplies. Against this background we examined methods of combating the likely emergence of shortages in Britain where blood is supplied entirely by donors.

No shortage in Britain?

When we first came to consider this problem we were struck by an assertion by the late Professor Richard M. Titmuss in his provocative pamphlet on social policy that, compared with the USA, which was occupied in a major war, 'in Britain, the situation is incomparably different. There is no shortage of blood'.[5] Since no evidence was offered to justify this remarkable state of affairs (we can think of very few desired objects without a price of which it can generally be said that there is no shortage), we undertook a small postal survey in 1968 which showed that 6 per cent of responding consultant surgeons

---

[4] Michael H. Cooper and Anthony J. Culyer, *The Price of Blood: an economic study of the charitable and commercial principle*, Hobart Paper 41, Institute of Economic Affairs, 1968. Also A. J. Culyer, 'Ethics and Economics in Blood Supply', *Lancet*, 20 March, 1970, pp. 602–603; 'Social Scientists and Blood Supply', *Lancet*, 11 July, 1970, pp. 1,247–8.

[5] Richard M. Titmuss, *Choice and 'the Welfare State'*, Fabian Tract 370, Fabian Society, London, p. 15; reprinted in *Commitment to Welfare*, Allen and Unwin, London, 1968.

considered blood supplies to their hospitals as 'poor' and that 36 per cent 'sometimes' had to postpone operations due to 'shortages' of blood.[6]

The major implications are, first, the desirability of more detailed inquiries than we were able to undertake and, secondly, that they tend to refute the assertion that 'there is no shortage'. Since we wrote our *Hobart Paper* (published in March 1968) there has been, to our knowledge, no more accurate analysis of the British situation and so it still seems appropriate to investigate methods of increasing supply, regardless of its current state, on the assumption of an accelerating upward trend in the demand for human blood. A revolution in the attitude of the public or in medical technology is possible, but growing pressure on supply seemed more likely than these rather optimistic alternatives. Moreover, serious shortages certainly exist elsewhere and in this essay we shall indicate some of the possible means of tackling them from the supply side.

Previous conclusions

In our 1968 *Paper*, precise meanings were attached to the inherently difficult concepts of 'need', 'adequacy' and 'shortages', which can otherwise be easily used to obfuscate the true issues and blind society to the choices it must make. We concluded that if reliance on donation alone failed to provide adequate supplies, the offer of a price to potential donors, whether in cash or in kind (a reciprocal gift from society) to compensate for inconvenience, or to persuade them to overcome natural apprehension, would be effective and morally and socially preferable to shortages, with their risk of avoidable deaths. Further, since supply from medically-eligible donors is a function not only of 'price' (in the sense of compensation) but also of information, distance, family size and other factors, attracting them by advertising, provision of transport and baby-sitting services, etc., would also be effective, but that choice between these methods (or combinations) ought to be made in terms of the social costs incurred by each in obtaining a given increase in the annual supply. Finally, we argued that, in general, it seemed likely that a combination of the donation sector, largely organised as it currently is, together with a separate system, possibly also run by the National Blood Transfusion Service, but which offered compensation,

[6] *The Price of Blood, op. cit.*, Table I, pp. 18–19.

would be the most effective and flexible method of ensuring adequate supplies.

III. THE OPPOSING VIEW

In *The Gift Relationship*,[7] Titmuss replied at length to our analysis and proposals. More precisely, he replied to his own interpretation of our argument while asking extremely important wider questions.

The Titmuss theory

Titmuss's position was that blood is not an economic commodity which should be bought and sold in the market. He supported it by describing in detail the characteristics of blood (for example, its perishability) that make it different from other commodities:[8] 'The very thought of blood, individual blood, touches the deepest feelings in man about life and death' (p. 16). Blood is deeply entrenched in man's belief and attitudes, he maintained, using extracts from the Bible and elsewhere in support.[9] Blood should be freely given and man's right to give blood should not be endangered by a market:

> 'Should men be free to sell their blood? Or should this freedom be curtailed to allow them to give or not to give blood?'[10] (p. 13)

He described world-wide shortages in the USA and elsewhere but

---

[7] Richard M. Titmuss, *The Gift Relationship: from human blood to social policy*, Allen and Unwin, London, 1970.

[8] A general refutation of the view espoused by Titmuss and many other social scientists, including economists, that medical care in general is so 'special' that some forms of production and distribution are inherently superior to others, is in A. J. Culyer, 'The Nature of the Commodity "Health Care" and its Efficient Allocation', *Oxford Economic Papers*, July 1971, pp. 189–211.

[9] Superstitions about blood occupy much of the Titmuss thesis. Similar beliefs have been, and are, held about human labour, buildings, wheels, vertical pieces of wood and stone, fire and a variety of every-day traded commodities. The trivial point seems to be worth making that superstitions are superstitions, and even if they are ubiquitous they are changeable by education and common sense. Blood, however, like human tissue, is significantly different from other objects of superstition. These more serious aspects are discussed below. In non-literate societies it may be that superstitions are not dysfunctional. In advanced societies they are, we would hold, mostly dysfunctional or irrelevant for improving social conditions. Many other social conventions (such as the gift-relationship, indeed!) perform the residual function of providing social cement at least as effectively as irrational beliefs about this and that and are, moreover, more useful in a direct sense as well as crediting humanity with a dignified intelligence.

[10] We find it difficult to appreciate the sense in which a man's freedom is curtailed when his options are extended. In one sense, he is free from having to make the choice, of course! But this is to say merely that he is free from being free.

considered there was no significant problem in Britain. He condemned our suggestion that prices or compensation might one day be offered in Britain as one method of increasing supplies by describing the failings of the American 'mixed' system, especially since the unprecedented demands of the Vietnam War, and associating all these failings with the American commercial blood-banks and in turn with all 'commercial' blood-banks, even those not operated in any obvious sense 'for profit'.

He concluded:

'From our study of the private market in blood in the US we have concluded that commercialisation of blood and donor relationships represses the expression of altruism, erodes the sense of community, lowers scientific standards, limits both personal and professional freedoms, sanctions the making of profits in hospitals and clinical laboratories, legalises hostility between doctor and patient, subjects critical areas of medicine to the laws of the market place, places immense social costs on those least able to bear them—the poor, the sick and the inept—increases the danger of unethical behaviour in various sectors of medical science and practice, and results in situations in which proportionally more and more blood is supplied by the poor, the unskilled, the unemployed, Negroes and other low-income groups and categories of exploited human populations of high blood yielders' (pp. 245–6).

Is altruism enough?

The American situation clearly leaves an enormous amount to be desired,[11] but the very existence of a 'commercial' sector in the USA suggests that altruism alone is not enough to ensure adequacy. No-one offers a price for a commodity or service readily available *gratis*—least of all in the USA. Can it seriously be supposed that removal of the 'commercial' sector in the USA would not result in enormous human suffering and aggravation of the admitted inadequacies? The contrast between a romantic vision of how things might be if only people were not as they are and the acute need for effective social reform could scarcely be stronger. It is important to distinguish between the two.

If altruism has been less successful in the US than in Britain (and, given the substantial differences in demand—Britain was not engaged in a major war—this is not obvious), it would be instructive to know

[11] While some of the defects itemised here do appear to be due to the commercialism of American blood-banking—and they are quite enough (in our view) to condemn the system as presently operated—it is very hard to show that others are attributable to it. Far more research (and definition of terms) is needed to infer erosion of the sense of community and reduction in scientific standards. Moreover, American blood-banking cannot 'sanction' profit-making hospitals, as Titmuss argued.

why. In his book (pp. 174–5) Titmuss presented a table of 27 countries which, together with Britain, comprise all those for which he could obtain information, showing that Britain is alone in not providing financial incentives (or compensation). This appears to be such a remarkable situation that it demanded an explanation (preferably testable for accuracy). But it received none.

Our fundamental criticism of the Titmuss approach is that its interesting vision of a just society was continuously mixed up with inconsequential assertions about social policy. He slipped throughout from discussions of what ought to be to assertions about what will be, from moral condemnations of what is to statements about how to make things better. But designing a better world requires some knowledge of how men will act if the constraints that affect behaviour are altered. On careful reading, Titmuss did not tell us how to reach the promised land.

The Titmuss facts

The major factual conclusions of Titmuss's book are:

1. There is no shortage of blood in Britain;
2. The US system has shown that 'private economic markets'[12] lead to:

   (a) waste; (b) substantial adverse externalities;[13] (c) shortages; (d) inflated GNP; (e) increased disease.

Titmuss's use of evidence appeared to be directed against a view (certainly not held by us nor anyone else so far as we know) that Britain ought to adopt the American system of blood collection and distribution. Consequently, the picture conjured up is that of the instant importability into Britain of all the American ills.

Shortage

Whether or not *serious* shortages exist in Britain remains unclear. The only possible objective stance is to remain sceptical. But the assertion that 'no' shortage at all exists is false. Quantitative data on demand are non-existent. No inference can be drawn from the 'fact' that British annual blood donations rose by 77 per cent between 1956

12 We do not appreciate the significance of the two adjectives.

13 He persistently confused adverse externalities with social costs. The latter embrace the former, for social costs include *all* costs. External costs are those not borne by the individual 'causing' them.

and 1967 compared with an 8 per cent rise in eligible donor population. Demand may have increased more, less or the same as the 77 per cent increase in supply. Still less meaningful is to compare this rate of growth in Britain with a 17 per cent rise in blood supply and a 16 per cent rise in eligible donor population over a slightly shorter time-period in the US. To be in the least significant such rates of increase must be related to the same base year levels of supply *and* demand and to the rate at which supply has already increased and is likely to increase. Even supposing that the rate of growth of generosity in the US is slower than in the UK, it is somewhat naïve to attribute this is the commercialisation of blood markets. Correlations do not establish cause and effect. Perhaps relative ungenerosity breeds commercialism, not the other way round. Many other hypotheses could also be entertained but not one received Titmuss's attention. Instead we have a mass of facts in search of an explanation.

In contrast to the situation in Britain, Titmuss found ample evidence of shortages in the US. The evidence he provided was the view of an American observer that operations are frequently postponed.[14]

The use of such casual evidence did not prevent Titmuss from dismissing our survey of consultant opinion as 'some allegations of shortage' (footnote, page 45). Comparable data relating to the US would, one suspects, have been held easily sufficient to show the American system's appalling inadequacy.

'Waste'—desirable and undesirable

The claim that the proportion of whole blood wasted in the US vastly exceeds that in Britain must also be suspect and at best is only suggestive, for it is not clear precisely why there is relatively so much more waste in the US. Failure to define 'waste' in a socially meaningful way also detracts attention from the apparently paradoxical but

---

[14] Evidence on 'wastage' defined in technological, rather than social, terms is more authoritatively presented, but how it relates to the profit-motive or to prices is not clear. Few American hospitals operate for profit, so why should hospitals there waste more than they do here? Could it be that *absence* of profit removes an incentive for many banks and many hospitals to co-operate and reduce inefficiency? And if some blood banks do operate for profit, why should they engage in waste? Perhaps they do not really try to make profits very hard. Perhaps the market is not as free as Titmuss suggested. Some explanation is called for, though he did not supply it. There is, of course, also the technical problem of matching seasonal rises and falls in demand and supply, a problem in efficient stock-holding for the medical operations research people or economists.

important proposition that some 'waste' is socially desirable. How much we cannot tell because of data deficiencies, though it seems clear that some exists in all countries, whether of blood put to no clinical use, to wrong clinical use, or held as a buffer stock. To prevent waste is itself costly. Wholly to eliminate it would almost certainly not be in society's best interests.[15] Even with adequate data showing the proportions of human blood 'wasted' in different countries, it could not be asserted that the country with the lowest percentage was less efficient. The assertion would require detailed knowledge of the rates and variance of demand and supply, the state of technical knowledge, the level of technology applicable, as well as a comprehensive and rigorous definition of 'waste'.

Suppose society places such a high value on the health of individuals that it maintains sufficient local stocks of whole blood, of *all* groups, to meet *all* demands at *all* times. A substantial quantity of whole blood would not, in practice, be used in transfusions for most of the time. This gap between units collected and transfused, which Titmuss used as a surrogate for 'administrative waste' in the US, might, even allowing for aged blood processed to yield useful blood derivatives, be a relevant concept of waste for some technical purposes. In an economic sense it would clearly not be waste, since society places a high value on the availability of the blood in banks. Wastage should not therefore (for policy purposes) be defined in the way Titmuss defined it. What is required is a complicated assessment of the relative (social) costs of keeping blood in a bank and in contactable donors, the value of additional contingency stocks, the costs of enforcing strict care in handling blood, and so on. For all these reasons crude international estimates of 'wastage' have no meaning. In any case, our conclusions were not predicated on any assertion that inducements to suppliers, or shadow pricing to hospitals, would be borrowing American methods and hence importing American problems.

Cost

Far more serious are other inferences Titmuss drew from his data. Our

---

15 Oddly, although precise technical definitions of 'waste' and 'shortage' appropriate to social choice are provided in our *Hobart Paper*, Titmuss rebuked us for not defining the latter concept in our little questionnaire (where we, like he, left it to the doctors to decide) and then failed himself to relate any of his own evidence to any clear definition. His evidence on waste was bedevilled by the lack of respectable data before the formation in 1967 of the National Blood Resource Program. He did not report on the results since its establishment.

Hobart Paper pointed to the danger of naïve cost comparisons. What is to be inferred from the statement that the cost per unit of blood is £10–£20 in the United States and £2 in Britain? Apart from the difficulty of comparing values expressed in different currencies, the external social costs (elsewhere emphasised by Titmuss) are completely ignored: time off work, unaccounted advertising costs, time waiting to donate, the risk (by no means negligible) of painful bruising, fear of an unspecified kind, etc. Moreover, unit costs depend on the rate of supply—zero supplies will certainly imply zero costs—and the relevant cost is at some optimal rate of supply. But who is to say that what is optimal in Britain will be optimal in Peru or in the US—even supposing there was some way of knowing whether Britain currently has an optimal rate? We are not asserting that Titmuss was wrong in saying that the British method is less costly in some relevant sense; but he did not present any evidence that it *is* less costly. Moreover, it is the change in total (i.e. *marginal*) cost of increasing supply, not the *average* unit cost, that is relevant in deciding which methods to employ to induce further increments in supply. International comparisons of unit costs are entirely irrelevant. But the costs of getting *additional* supplies are even harder to know than the unit costs of current supplies.

The whole question of shortage and waste requires to be considered in a far wider context. If postponement of surgical operations is one indicator of shortage (it must not be identified with shortage itself), other aspects also warrant attention. To what extent is blood employed where other more valuable uses exist? To what extent are limitations on the expected quantity in the future partly (and perhaps only implicitly) assumed as given in planning the provision of blood-intensive medical care? Buildings, manpower and mechanical equipment are thought the major constraints on wider provision for people's 'needs', but blood too is scarce and is likely to become increasingly so. The economist must ask, every time an eligible patient is denied renal dialysis, whether the difficulty of ensuring enough blood, without depriving others, plays any part in such decisions (or the prior ones that make them inevitable). Blood, as one of many scarce medical resources, must not be considered only as having a demand derived from purely medical considerations today. There is also a 'complementary demand' derived from the availability of complementary inputs as determined by past decisions. There is at least the possibility that expectations about tomorrow's supply of blood may affect today's supply of other inputs and hence tomorrow's demand for blood, making it appear falsely low when tomorrow arrives.

Another dimension of adequacy worth pursuing concentrates on the composition of supply rather than its total. In particular, though not all patients need blood only of their type, some British patients undoubtedly receive blood imperfectly matched. Theoretically, AB patients ought to get AB blood, but since it is relatively scarce they are frequently given A. This is safe since the patient will not make anti-A antibodies if he has some A red cells. Group B is also scarce; so the patients may receive group O blood, which is sometimes unsafe. Sometimes Rhesus Negative patients have to receive Rhesus Positive blood. This is definitely risky and quite unjustifiable in a young woman or girl who may make antibodies and be unable to bear Rhesus Positive babies, but the risk seems to be accepted from time to time in males or elderly patients. Research into the frequency with which patients of one type are given blood of another would provide another dimension to the discussion of shortage. We are not so complacent as to imagine that such inquiries are unnecessary.

Inflation

Another fallacy concerns the alleged 'inflation' of GNP if hitherto unpaid services are paid for. It is the practice to 'inflate' GNP figures by 'shadow pricing' some important unpaid services (such as those derived from their houses by owner-occupiers). But the GNP is only a (crude) statistical approximation to the flow of value created by a society. That it misses much (and certainly almost all the most important things in civilised life) and includes much as well (every time we miss the bus and take a taxi, GNP rises) teaches caution in using such data, but not to be concerned about including real services previously omitted. The real error here is a failure to understand the two-way flow that characterises exchange procedures. That a service is *given* ('free') implies an increase in general well-being. Well-being will not normally be reduced if the same flow is paid for voluntarily: indeed, it may remain the same (if the cash payment is treated solely as a transfer) or it may even increase when payment has the (usual) effect of increasing the supply. The Titmuss view that the provision of blood by the poorer members of society for the richer was a regressive transfer failed to account of the corresponding flow of money or real resources from the rich to the poor as compensation. Indeed, if there is as large an excess demand for blood in, say, the US as he alleged, with an inflation of its supply price (in money or any other terms), the more plausible inference is that the poor are getting a more than equal share in the mutual gains from exchanging whole blood. This does not seem significantly relevant to the question of how to organise blood collection and distribution but, insofar as it *is*, it seems most unlikely to be regressive.

The hepatitis risk

As Titmuss rightly pointed out, there exists a well-established link between the contraction of often fatal hepatitis in recipients with use of 'professional' donors, especially if black, poor or belonging to the section of society most lacking in affection and in most urgent need of housing and more medical, nutritional, educational and financial support. But is it the price that causes the disease or the poverty? Clearly it is not the price *per se*.[16] How then can an exchange system be devised that might avoid the problem?

The following set of possibilities derives from our earlier analysis of blood supply.

1. Assume no clinical test in the foreseeable future will enable carriers of viral hepatitis to be identified before blood donation (this assumption will later be relaxed). The following policy actions are now possible:

(a) collect all blood, including infected, and distribute as usual on the grounds that it is better to incur a risk (not a certainty) that recipients contract hepatitis than increasing the risk of getting no blood at all because of exacerbated shortages. This is the wrong policy (we think) since better choices are available. It is a valid criticism of the American system that it has largely adopted this policy.

(b) Offer a price sufficiently high to produce an excess supply of donors from amongst whom to choose those with the desired characteristics as evidenced by dress, occupation, education, etc. This policy may be too costly, though there may evidently be circumstances in which the value of additional whole blood is sufficient to warrant the high costs. If discrimination of this

[16] The question would be silly were it not that the continuous word-associations used by Titmuss require us to rebut this association, and were it not also that the answer produces a variety of means of mitigating the incidence of the disease which have been missed throughout *The Gift Relationship*. M. Reddin, in a scurrilous letter in *Lancet*, took exception to this 'disingenuous' question and proceeded to ignore its implications ('Economics of Blood Supply', *Lancet*, 8 May, 1971)—suggesting that a little 'disingenuity' may not be unproductive.

type is regarded as socially undesirable, the present British system, to the extent that it avoids viral hepatitis carriers, also implicitly discriminates in some of these ways. Of course, implicit discrimination may be preferred to explicit.[17]

(c) Discriminate in the collection market by offering prices only to pre-chosen categories, for example, university students and teachers, members of the armed forces, office workers, residents of well-to-do districts. Such discrimination is clearly costly but may be worthwhile under conditions of shortage.

(d) Offer a 'price' *in kind* of such a sort that it would tend to appeal to the appropriate social class of supplier, for example, West End theatre tickets, bigger certificates of donation, free parking vouchers or piano lessons, a bottle of burgundy. This policy is not costless and would tend to work better the less easy it was to sell the 'gift'.

2. Retain a donation-only system and encourage collection by advertising, jogging consciences, public lectures on ethics, reducing the costs of attendance (e.g. by providing baby-sitting services, rewarding firms that free workers for attendance, improving the scheduling programme at donor sessions, etc.). In short, increase supply by varying all or some of its *non-price* determinants. None of these methods is costless. In particular, we suspect the Americans might doubt the efficacy of this set of methods as the solution to their problem.

3. There have been significant advances in blood transfusion in recent years (in particular Blumberg's discovery of the Australia antigen and its linking by Prince with serum hepatitis).* The techniques deriving from these discoveries such as cross-over electropheresis will, within a few years, almost certainly make of post-transfusion hepatitis no more than an old nightmare like the scourges of the great infectious diseases, minimising the risk associated with simplistic price systems and hence much of the Titmuss case against them. Screening against serum hepatitis is being adopted in the all-donor British system. Like the other methods of minimising the incidence of this disease these also are not costless.

---

[17] In *The Price of Blood*, p. 26, we hypothesised that the supply of gifts is income-elastic. This view was fortunately supported by Titmuss's questionnaire to blood donors among whom social classes I and II were over-represented and classes IV and V under-represented compared with the general eligible population.

* Discussed by Dr A. J. Salsbury in his medical evidence, below, pp. 179–191.

The choice facing society

We may therefore conclude this section by itemising the key elements in the choice that confronts every country in the nature of the collection and transfusion of blood. The intensity of each of these problems varies from place to place, partly due to its stage of economic development (wealthy countries can afford better technology and place higher values on human life), partly to transitory circumstances affecting demand (war or peace, for example), and partly also, we suspect, to the attitudes that individuals have to one another (the propensity to give and the motives for giving vary from culture to culture).

In every country more blood is desired for direct and indirect clinical uses. To increase supplies one may use donation and/or pricing methods. Currently, at least in the US, it would appear that donation needs to be supplemented by prices to meet demand. But the more prices are used the higher the risk of disease transmission through transfusion (or through disease associated with transfusion). The choice may thus, at its simplest, be seen as between less blood of high average quality and more of lower quality. The real choice is more complicated than this for, *at a cost*, pricing schemes can be devised which reduce the risk of disease. Indeed donation alone, with sufficient advertising and facilitating amenities to ease donor attendances, might *at a cost* produce adequate supplies. Moreover, investment in screening may soon, *at a cost*, reduce the risk of disease to very low levels.

Titmuss plumped for straight donation. This *may* be adequate for Britain, though in other countries, particularly the US, it is surprising that he prescribed an all-or-none solution. If donation were the only method of blood collection permitted in the US it would be rash indeed to predict that shortage would be reduced. But, if not, what value is being placed upon the lives of patients lost through devotion to the principle of donation?—lower, one suspects, than the patients would. Alternatively, suppose that by massive public campaigns the rate of donation could be permanently doubled (or trebled) and a shortage eliminated. Would society really be prepared to foot the bill? It may, or it may not.

The truth is that society does not usually take the all-or-none view. It is not absolutely averse to taking risks, for they are costly to avoid. We may be prepared, when costs are high, to tolerate a degree of risk of infection through transfusion. We are prepared, at lower cost levels, to tolerate some unsatisfied demands. We are probably even prepared to sacrifice the noble principle of giving as an end in order to use more commercial methods to achieve another, clinical, end.

We repeat the *Hobart Paper* view that there is no *a priori* means of choosing the best method of organising blood supplies in a world where moral absolutes are not unique and do not reign supreme. The best depends, in practice, on society's objectives, the conflicts between them, and the costs of alternative means of attaining them. For these reasons we argued that payment for blood *may* be both sensible and humane—though it may be neither necessary nor desirable. The answer depends entirely upon the circumstances. But it is clear also that many of the worst consequences of 'commercialism' can be reduced by the imaginative control of 'markets'. It is, however, possible to discuss these problems and their possible solutions only if the fundamental Titmuss assertion—that blood is not an economic good—is decisively rejected.

IV. THE ECONOMIC THEORY OF BLOOD DONATION

The fundamental theorem

Economics is traditionally associated with the study of the exchange of scarce goods and services between persons for goods and services or claims to goods and services in the form of money. To concentrate upon such formal trading in markets is to exclude much human behaviour of importance in questions of, for example, social policy. In this section we explore the economic theory of donation and find that some of its many implications lend further support to the plausibility of our earlier arguments. The theory is not a 'moral' theory of human action: it simplifies quite dramatically what we know in truth to be very complex processes. It is one of the simplest general theories of these complex processes but it *does* explain events and it *can* be tested. It is therefore potentially useful. That is our sole justification for using it.[18]

We shall assume throughout that human behaviour is predictable, a necessary condition, needless to say, for the existence of social science. More specifically we shall assume that this predictability

---

[18] The analysis in this section follows that of Professors Armen Alchian and William Allen in their perceptive discussion of 'philanthropy' in *Exchange and Production: Theory in Use*, Wadsworth, Belmont, 1969, Ch. 8. [This book is a shortened version of the authors' *University Economics*; the extract is reproduced in revised form in Part I, Essay 1.]

derives from the conformity of individual (or 'representative' individual) behaviour with the axioms of modern utility-maximising theory. In this section we shall build upon the basic but general approach in the essays by Alchian and Allen and by Culyer in Part I to work towards a theory of blood donation.

At any moment of time, the utility-maximising theory postulates that the chosen collection of desired goods or services is such that, provided nothing else changes, he will not choose any alternative collection. This may sound tautological, but it is not the same as saying that people go on doing what they are doing until they feel inclined to stop. For if it is possible to specify some of the objects in the chosen collection (which will be easy since choices almost invariably have observable consequences) we can infer the (non-tautological) demand theorem: the more a person must sacrifice of one object to acquire more of another, the less of the other he will take.

Who gains from gifts?

The generality of this fundamental inference enables us to proceed immediately with an analysis of giving. A gift is defined as presenting someone with an object at a contractual price deliberately less than the market price. ('Contractual' in the sense that the receiver is required to pay something, not necessarily money, in exchange.) A donor may, of course, sometimes hope to get something in exchange from the other person,[19] but the hope is not a contract. If the contractual price is zero, we have a 'pure' or 'free' gift, but the concept of giving is not confined to *wholly* free gifts. To provide an object at a partial (less than market) price does not destroy or remove the quality of charity. A second aspect of a gift is that the beneficiary shall be prevented by contract, courtesy, custom or technology from re-selling it.

Some elementary economics of giving can be conveniently expounded using the familiar apparatus of demand. The bulk of this analysis can be found in Appendix A (page 139), which also outlines the assumptions underlying the propositions in the rest of this section. This analysis helps to explain why gifts frequently take the form they

[19] Such as another gift, love, loyalty, indebtedness. In our analysis, however, we are supposing that individuals are genuinely altruistic (at least, to a degree). Alternative, more realistic, assumptions about the motivations of those who give are more complex than we need for our purposes and would not, in any case, change our conclusions so long as we are correct in believing that people are, at least sometimes, genuinely unselfish.

do and to predict some of the consequences of changing the nature of the relationship between the given (donor) and the recipient (donee). In particular, we can investigate the theoretical assertion that 'commercialism' represses 'altruism'.

The general case can be described by imagining a world of two individuals—the giver and the recipient. We shall consider also a case lying between an outright sale and an outright (free) gift, that is, where the giver makes a gift at a less than market price. The costs and benefits to the two individuals may then be derived if we know:

(a) how much the recipient would have spent on the commodity if it had not been given to him;
(b) the cost of the gift to the recipient;
(c) the total value to the recipient of the gift;
(d) the total value to the recipient of the alternative amount of the commodity he would have obtained;
(e) the total value placed by the giver upon the amount he gives;
(f) the market value of the gift.

The difference between (a) and (b) (the difference in the recipient's total expenditure) is an *effect in cash* which may leave him better or worse off than before, depending on relative expenditures.

The difference between (c) and (d) (the difference in the total value of the commodity owned by the recipient) is an *effect in kind* which will leave him better off than before.

The total gain to the recipient after the gift is measured by the sum of these two differences. It is equivalent to a gain in 'consumer's surplus' from consumption of the commodity. By definition, even if the cash effect is negative, the effect in kind must outweigh it to produce a net benefit to the recipient or he would not accept the gift. (We assume that gifts are not consumed compulsorily.)[20]

The cost to the donor is the difference between (e) and (f) (the total value placed by him on the gift less what he paid or would have to pay for it, or could sell it for). This is an *effect in kind* representing a loss to the donor of a specific resource. In addition, he loses the difference between (f) and (b) (the market value of the gift less what

[20] This assumption is sometimes falsified. British state education is provided as a 'gift' to parents of school-age children by the whole of society and some education must be consumed (arguably a partial gift insofar as parents pay for it by taxes). Some might argue the case for this 'merit' good being further refined so that *state* education would be compulsorily consumed by all.

he gets for it from the recipient). The total cost to the donor is the sum of these two differences.

The net cost to the donor is inexplicable if the traditional economic approach is taken as being founded upon an assumption of 'selfishness' or 'economic man'. On our less restrictive interpretation it can be explained as a cost accepted by the donor because he chooses to make the gift. And by a well-known principle of cost-benefit analysis, this accepted cost provides a *minimal* estimate of the intrinsic value of giving to the *donor*.[21]

This cost must exceed the net benefit to the recipient. The difference between the two (*conceptually* measured in monetary units) appears to be 'waste'—it is the value sacrificed by the giver but not received by the taker. For the donor it is not waste, since he chooses to make the gift. For the taker *some* of it is waste, for he would gain if he were permitted to resell the gift at its market value. Alternatively, he would be indifferent between a saleable gift and money equal to the market value of the gift if it could be resold (at no transaction or search cost, which is rare).

Some paradoxes of giving

If the recipient would prefer a saleable gift or equivalent money to the non-transferable gift, and if the giver would incur a smaller cost if he gave equivalent money (he would then not incur the loss in kind):

(a) why should the unsaleable gift be preferred by the donor?
(b) is not the gift relationship ultimately (and paradoxically) anti-social by promoting all-round social losses (costs).

The major explanation for (a) in terms of the analysis so far is that the donor's concern is to ensure that the taker receives not a gift of certain *value* but *the gift itself*.

This constitutes the fundamental reason why gifts (or 'transfers', as pure gifts are known in the literature of public finance) may be given in kind rather than in cash. Thus, people are given subsidised housing, 'free' health care, education, etc. rather than money equivalents to ensure that they consume the objects or services and do not spend the money on something else. This is a neutral ('be-

[21] It is a minimal estimate of the gain in consumers' surplus to the donor, for it canno be less than this and could generally be more. For a theoretical discussion of the principles of cost-benefit analysis, E. J. Mishan, *Cost-Benefit Analysis*, Allen and Unwin, 1971.

havioural') explanation deriving from givers' preferences ('utility functions'), not an ethical commentary on the relative desirability of types of gift.

On paradox (b), again several answers suggest themselves. One is consistent with the analysis so far: since gifts are voluntary acts between individuals we are essentially comparing two 'states of the world'—one in which neither giver nor taker gains utility because *no* gift is made and one in which both gain some utility because a gift *is* made. Since, presumably, the terms upon which a gift is made are negotiable between the two parties but many gifts continue in kind, the presumption must be that takers who would prefer a straight money transfer cannot compensate givers who prefer the non-transferable gift in kind to persuade them to change the gift from kind to money. The additional gains to recipients from money transfers must presumably therefore be less than the losses to the donors that would result from changing the form of the gift. (In cost-benefit analysis, these potential gains to recipients provide a *minimal* measure of the benefit to *donors* of gifts in kind relative to money equivalents.)

Further, although it is easy to argue that gift relationships have intrinsic social value above the intrinsic value (if any) of normal trading relationships, it is also possible to argue, on the contrary, that gift relationships frequently display socially undesired or undesirable characteristics such as paternalism, creation of a sense of obligation or dependence in the recipients, and so on. On these wider issues, economists have no technical competence, nor ethical or political authority; we suspect them, however, to be of major significance chiefly in primitive societies.

Some predictions of the theory

Several of the behavioural consequences of giving have been analysed by Professors Armen A. Alchian and William R. Allen.[22] Many implications of interest are discussed by them and by Culyer in Part I. A major result of our analysis thus far has been that the nature of the gift (and its amount) will be determined primarily by the *donor*.

---

[22] *Op. cit.*, pp. 168–172. That many gifts from the whole of society to individuals exhibit much 'publicness' (i.e. many people derive a benefit from a single donor's gift leads to some fascinating implications for public choice and for the design of governmental institutions. A suggestive introduction is Gordon Tullock, *Private Wants, Public Means: An Economic Analysis of the Desirable Scope of Government*, Basic Books, New York and London, 1970.

The recipient, insofar as he does not obtain a change in the form of the gift, is relevant only inasmuch as he derives a net benefit from its receipt, once the donor has decided what kind of gift to make and how much. Consequently people are sometimes disappointed by gifts.[23]

But how much will the donor give? The answer, of course, is 'he will give the amount that maximises his utility'. Utility-maximising behaviour implies that he will increase the size of gift (or frequency of giving) up to the size (or rate) at which the *disadvantages* of increasing the size by a small amount in terms of what is foregone would just be offset by the *advantages* of such a small increase (as he sees them). At any moment of time, the utility maximising hypothesis asserts that the donor's marginal utility[24] derived from making a gift is the same as the marginal loss of utility incurred by foregoing its consumption himself. This marginal loss is affected by whatever charge he makes. The important feature is that the marginal value of the gift *in the donor's own use* rises as he gives more away. Conversely, the assumptions imply that the marginal value to him of giving *for someone's use* falls as he gives more.

The chosen size of the gift or rate of giving is thus determined by the price at which the gift is made (for unselfish people, a zero price implies a positive amount of giving) and the donor's 'supply curve' of gifts.[25]

Finally, what determines the price charged for the gift? If the recipient's ability to pay does *not* enter the donor's preferences and

---

[23] A more complete analysis than that attempted here might include the recipient's *reaction* to a gift in the donor's utility function, especially for gifts between persons. For example, the probability of getting thanks, a smile, a kiss should certainly be included in a comprehensive analysis of inter-personal gifts.

[24] Specifically, for those who still suspect metaphysics in the utility concept, it is the marginal value of a unit of the gift in terms of some other (*numéraire*) commodity: the marginal trade-off between the two. Titmuss insisted upon the 'unquantifiable and unmethodical' (p. 224) aspects of problems as distinguishing 'social' from 'economic' policy. Since he nevertheless adopted a functionalist approach to the gift-relationship these adjectives would seem to imply that gift-relationships are *not* 'social' phenomena. He also specifically dissociated himself from the 'principles of marginal utility analysis' (pp. 211–212) but got the principles wrong. The analysis here *is* based on modern utility theory (a good introduction is V. Walsh, *Introduction to Contemporary Microeconomics*, McGraw-Hill, 1969), but its behavioural (non-normative) predictions could be equally derived from random or habitual choice-making by individuals (G. S. Becker, 'Irrational Behaviour and Economic Theory', *Journal of Political Economy*, 1962, pp. 1–13).

[25] The derivation of this curve is geometrically explained in Appendix A (p. 139), but it has essentially the same characteristics as all (upward-sloping) supply curves.

decisions, the price will be set so as to exhaust any net benefit the recipient may receive from the gift, and the price will be uniquely determined.[26] If, as may be more usual, such considerations do weigh with the donor, the price will be set lower than this—possibly at zero.

Is this approach really necessary?

This apparatus, though it may appear abstract, is necessary for the analysis of blood donation. It enables us to pinpoint some of the sources of recent controversy arising from our *Hobart Paper* and it indicates modifications to the *general* theory required to tailor it to blood. We differ fundamentally from Titmuss, who regarded such 'models' as 'irrelevant to an understanding of the place of blood in modern systems of medical care'.[27] Our model may be wrong, but it is hardly irrelevant, and we have yet to see any alternative offered explicitly that could be compared with it. He based his assertion on the premises that gifts in economic models must have 'exchange value' (our model does not depend upon (f) above taking a positive value); that they are a form of 'gift-exchange' or non-contractual barter (i.e. that a gift is made in expectation of a reciprocal reward, which we have specifically rejected though some gifts undoubtedly are made with such expectations); and that 'utility' is a 'metaphysical concept'. Each of these premises is generally false. 'Creative altruism' can be analysed with our framework and lies, indeed, at the heart of it. It exists, is important and can be analysed. So can the gift of human blood.

V. BLOOD AND THE ECONOMICS OF GIVING

In Britain, blood is given voluntarily and freely. There is no price. The rate of donation by people generous enough to give their blood has varied since 1948 between 1·03 and 1·33 per donor per year of about a million and a quarter donors.

Donors' response to prices

Our *Hobart Paper* assumed that the amount of blood supplied would not be sensitive to changes in the price offered, i.e. that positive

---

[26] For more detailed analysis, M. V. Pauly, 'Efficiency in the Provision of Consumption Subsidies', *Kyklos*, Vol. XXIII, 1970.

[27] *The Gift Relationship*, p. 213.

prices would not induce donors to supply more. The preceding analysis suggests that donors *would* respond to prices by supplying more than they do at zero price. The reason for our original assumption (no response to price) lay in the feeling (we had no empirical evidence) that the utility analysis of giving outlined above over-simplified the fundamental behaviour of donors by excluding *price itself* from their 'utility function'. We thought that the smack of 'commercialism' involved in paying suppliers might be off-putting.[28]

Subsequently the Titmuss evidence on the motivation of blood donors (although of the sort that seeks to explain behaviour by asking motives, which is notoriously unreliable especially if the questions encourage self-satisfaction) appeared to be that donors (6 per cent of the population) are largely motivated by a sincere desire to help other people. To the extent that it is true, this finding implies that our altruistic choice 'model' is an appropriate way of examining donors' behaviour. The Titmuss evidence encourages us to be less cautious in interpreting the response of donors to price or to a reciprocal gift, both of which reduce the disincentive in supplying more.[29]

Specious distinctions

Our analysis in Appendix B (p. 142) suggests there is something specious in making distinctions between 'kinds' of givers based on whether, for example, they give with the expectation of a reward or whether they perform 'acts of conscience without shame'.[30] If our fundamental hypothesis is correct—'the lower the cost the more the

[28] We also noted that the total supply elasticity might be *negative* (i.e. the curve slope backwards from right to left). A condition to avoid this possibility was that the sum of the price elasticities of supply from 'donors' and 'professional' suppliers exceeds zero. We now ensure this through the assumption in footnote 35, which Titmuss's evidence suggests may be *too weak* a description of reality.

[29] *The Gift Relationship*, pp. 226–236, 306–319. Nearly 80 per cent of the answers to his questionnaire suggest 'a high sense of social responsibility towards the needs of other members of the society. Perhaps this is one of the outstanding impressions which emerges from the analysis' (p. 319). He did not, unfortunately, incorporate a question designed to elicit a response concerning the donor's reactions to various forms of payment for their blood. Had the respondents then displayed marked intentions of withdrawing their gift, much of our fundamental theory would have been called in question (though not behaviourally refuted) as well as his own conclusions about their high sense of social responsibility. The question would then become one of the level of compensation at which new suppliers equalled withdrawing suppliers, for the supply curve would initially bend backwards and then upwards to the right.

[30] *The Gift Relationship*, p. 89.

activity'—from the *behavioural* point of view, such categorising[31] may, at best, provide explanations of the quantity of blood supplied and the slope of the supply curve. Categories and 'shopping lists' are useful only inasmuch as they identify (but no more) some influences that may determine behaviour, and upon which policy may operate to change it, or inasmuch as it is wished to award moral plaudits to people whose motives are judged the most agreeable. The morality of keeping to the horizontal axis in Fig. IV (p. 144) rather than operating in all the potential space bounded by it and the vertical axis is discussed in a later section (pp. 135–137). The conclusion is that, with prices, many suppliers are still more generous than others, even though all may, to the unsympathetic, be classified unkindly as 'professional' donors. In our view, the analytical position of free giving is at the opposite extreme along a continuum from selling an object for the maximum amount a person will pay for it.[32] Market exchange normally lies between these two extremes, and so does much giving.

VI. OBJECTIONS TO THE METHOD

The Titmuss objections to this kind of analysis, which does not differ fundamentally from that in the *Hobart Paper*, appeared to be:

1. It obscures the distinction between the 'social' and the 'economic' in social policy. (*The Gift Relationship*, Ch. 12, *passim*.)
2. It denies that 'ethics' come before 'economics' (p. 208).
3. It is crudely utilitarian (p. 195).
4. Its implications for policy imply that 'the utilities of different persons are empirically comparable'.

Objections refuted

Each of these objections is based upon a misrepresentation of the arguments.

1. Simple definitions of 'social' and 'economic' problems do not exist. Any social problem has many dimensions. For blood, there are religious, political, sociological, economic, medical, ethical facets,

31 This demonstrates, we believe, the profound scientific weakness of categorising actions, events, etc., in the absence of any theory of behaviour. Such categories 'explain' nothing, do not aid understanding, least of all do they permit prediction.

32 This amount normally exceeds the market price and is the amount potentially to be exacted by a perfectly discriminating monopolist who fully exploits his monopoly (and his customers!).

and others. It would be not only unwise but also futile to try to eliminate any of them. The economic aspect of blood supply and demand derives from the 'social need' for adequate blood supplies. Therefore we must face and try to settle these questions: How is blood supplied and distributed? How do we tell what supply is 'enough'? How is it rationed? How financed? What predictable effects do the current social institutions produce? What effects would follow if they were altered? All these questions are of public or 'social' concern: to separate 'economic' from 'social' is analogous to separating 'sociological' or 'medical' or 'political' from 'social'—not a promising endeavour. It is rather unlikely that one could arrive at satisfactory answers to mistaken questions. What makes each of these disciplinary labels different is the *methods* used, not the subject matter studied. And each will normally have something useful to contribute.

2. Economics does not, insofar as there is any meaning in the allegation, come 'before' ethics. *Only* the ends can justify the means—and economics is about the means. Some means may be inconsistent with the ends (perhaps this is what Titmuss was trying to say). And some means may be impossible to justify by *any* ends. But if the end is to ensure 'adequate' blood supplies, there exists a by no means simple or obvious choice of means or combination of means. Even if the ends are extended to incorporate the principle of charity (in its undebased sense), there is still a variety of means, and choice is made even more complex because the two ends (adequate supplies and the preservation of an ethical principle) may conflict with each other.

3. Titmuss misrepresented the meaning of modern utility-maximising theory. As social scientists we take the view that the theory is appropriate insofar as it is refutable but unrefuted by events. Nowhere in *The Gift Relationship* were data presented to refute the theory; so we feel no obligation to modify it or to substitute an alternative. The Titmuss theory of giving (in Chs. 5, 12 and 13) was really a variety of conversational explanations that provided no scientific means by which they might have been distinguished nor how they might have been falsified. Instead, he objected to some of the sociological literature on the grounds that not all kinds of gifts are considered. The core of the Titmuss theory was that the

> 'forms and functions of giving . . . may reflect, sustain, strengthen or loosen the cultural bonds of the group, large or small' (p. 71).

This is not the kind of theory that social scientists can accept at all. It has no testable implications. Giving may, indeed, do any of these things. No conceivable events in the real world could be inconsistent with this view—it explains everything and therefore nothing.

The following page (p. 72) reveals all. Titmuss's major concern was to borrow from Marcel Mauss the use of the customs and practices of 'non-economic' (*sic*) giving as an *indicator* of the 'texture of personal and group relationships in different cultures'. The extent and manner of giving in society thus became a romantic measure of Titmuss's degree of approval of various societies. The Titmuss ethical views of different societies have been of interest. The ethical coin, however, became somewhat debased by the use of the proposition about the 'texture' and 'fabric' of society as a pseudo-scientific device. From it he drew the one, unique, positive implication of his theory. This comes much later (p. 199):

> 'If the bonds of community giving are broken the result is not a state of value neutralism. The vacuum is likely to be filled by hostility and social conflict'.

As a general proposition this is a remarkably bold prediction, not derived logically (so far as we can see) from the theories of giving he provided nor, we suspect, sustained by evidence (he provided none).

What is even more remarkable is that this prediction occurs in the middle of a section discussing exchanging blood for dollars. It is almost beyond belief that the introduction of payment (in some form) for blood supplies in Britain would provoke 'hostility and social conflict'. We find it hard to believe even that the doctor-patient relationship would be harmed by it. Yet this is what pseudo-science would apparently have us believe!

It is, perhaps, not surprising that these fallacies are to be found extensively in the early anthropological literature upon which Titmuss drew heavily. To most people it must appear dangerous to draw inferences about the functions of social activities in *primitive* societies and apply them at a broad level to other cultures, especially the more complex modern cultures with which we are concerned, which have different technologies, values and objectives and, moreover, a much wider diversity of all of them.

4. The attack on normative interpretations of 'utility' is not only mistaken; it is also mischievous in that it fails to acknowledge that 'economists' in discussing the blood 'market' explicitly rejected the Paretian framework anyway.[33]

[33] He seems also (p. 206) to have identified 'consumer sovereignty' with 'Pareto-

VII. ETHICS AND THE FUNCTION OF GIVING IN SOCIAL POLICY

The economics of giving suggests some general ways in which, if more blood is needed, supplies could be increased. It also suggests ways which may be of use not only in Britain but also, with more current urgency, perhaps, in other countries such as the US. We detect no such fruitful implications in the alternative way of looking at the problem suggested by Titmuss. Indeed, his contribution provided neither a guideline for adoption in overseas blood markets nor a prescription capable of being applied to other goods or services. Why should the role of altruism be applied only to blood? What of other fields of human endeavour? What of other avenues for giving? Why has the disappearance of voluntary hospitals no implications for 'hostility and social conflict'? Or is there a difference between gifts from individual to individual, from the individual to the collectivity, and from the collectivity to the individual? For blood, some of the methods suggested in the *Hobart Paper* would use a price or a reciprocal gift. Others would operate on the non-price determinants of supply. Sensible policy would be based on the estimated relative social costs of these alternative methods in procuring a given supply. In practice we have no very good idea of the true social costs and even less of the responsiveness of suppliers' behaviour to given changes in demand. They can be found only by trial and error.

Is there not something *immoral* about paying people for their blood? Is there not something fundamentally *good* about gifts from the individual to an anonymous collectivity? Many would say emphatically that there is, in each case. Their argument might be paraphrased: the good society is anonymously altruistic, altruism must be learned, if altruism is to be learned and practised the opportunities must be provided by social institutions created by social policies. Here we confront an apparently irresolvable ends-means problem.

Obviously, nobody will dispute that altruism is to be desired (it is clearly good to be good), but it is only unambiguously desirable as a

---

optimality'. As a matter of fact, Paretian economics assumes no one person, or class, to be 'sovereign'—neither consumers, nor producers, nor even planners. Pareto-optimality means that the well-being of any person cannot be further improved without adversely affecting another person after all feasible compensations have taken place. It is not the same thing as a dictatorship of consumers (consumer sovereignty) or dictatorship of the proletariat or any other group in society.

personal trait. It is certainly not unambiguously good as a general legislative or institutional feature. Thus, while the freedom to give is elemental, of which our society may be proud, it is not obviously desirable that public policy should be predicated upon the freedom to give and *only* to give. This would be to *force* people to give and may have immeasurably harmful effects upon the well-being of society. Moral absolutism of this sort would be ready to contenance the unnecessary death of a patient denied transfusions and the benefit of other blood-based products in a system with only the 'freedom' to be altruistic but where people were singularly selfish. Man does not live by altruism alone, and altruism as an *end* can conflict with its desirability as a *means*. As economists would say in their unbeautiful (but practical) language: there is a trade-off problem. (There is also a philosophical problem, for the morality of apparently virtuous actions performed without choice must be in question.)

If your freedom is to stop at the end of our nose, as the least libertarian of social scientists would agree it should, you must also have another right—to sell, so that we can compensate you for parting with something you own which we desire but which you choose not to give. The original *Hobart Paper* apparatus viewed *both* procedures—giving and selling—as *complementary* methods of generating blood supplies. The argument was not based upon these wider ethical considerations but it can also be defended on such grounds. The economist's question will be: *How much* of that desired object, an altruistic society, can we afford to sacrifice? But it is not for him to answer the question on society's behalf, nor is it for the social administrator, nor the medical practitioner. It is a question for the whole of society since it affects the whole of society, and in this all our individual voices are but a few among millions.[34] The social scientist's task is to ascertain the facts and to present the alternative courses of action for society's representatives to chose. There is no reason why

[34] The loss of altruism (if it exists at all) is the major social cost in the Titmuss critique of our proposals. We are not impressed with Titmuss's case for its existence on any significant scale in blood supplies and, as we have also emphasised, the determination of its size, even in a qualitative way, is not for social scientists to decide. For these reasons, it had not occurred to us to discuss this problem in the *Hobart Paper*. Oddly enough, Titmuss chastised cost-benefit analysts for supposing that unquantifiable costs and benefits must always be small (but they do not as a rule—at least the better ones do not) while he, with equal lack of justification, supposed them to be big. As our analysis (pp. 130–131) shows, altruism may in practice be harder to observe than is commonly supposed (which is not to say that it does not exist nor that it is unimportant). Cf. also Culyer's essay (No. 3) in Part I where the notion of altruism receives finer surgery.

zero-price giving should not remain and be *supplemented* by a paying sector—depending on the costs. It is simply not *necessary* to deny anyone the *opportunity* to give, not because of extravagant and unsupported speculations about the collapse of community life but because of the practical function of blood *donation* in meeting immediate needs.

VIII. CONCLUSIONS

In general, both our own further analysis and new information confirm the conclusions reached in the *Hobart Paper*. There is good reason to suppose that blood supplies would be responsive in the right direction if payment were offered. The degree of responsiveness could be discovered only by trial. It is easy to define wholly inadequate criteria by which to assess the adequacy, or otherwise, of current supplies and to evaluate the seriousness of shortage and waste. In practice, we would not expect usable criteria to fulfil all the desirable criteria we have discussed, but is is dangerous to make comparisons over time, or internationally, without an awareness of these factors.

If other countries have been successful in operating payment systems, in money or kind, in the sense that they appear to have increased annual supplies above what they otherwise would have been, it is also clear that our analysis indicates some of the ways in which the disadvantages of these methods (such as the hepatitis risk) may be reduced or almost certainly eliminated (*no* system—even the NHS—has so far managed to reduce the risk to zero). We do not pretend to know what kinds and degrees of risk of this sort are to be regarded as socially acceptable. Such decisions must plainly be determined by the value society places on reducing such risks; and much depends on the social cost of reducing them. The former is not infinite. The latter is not zero. But we have little information at this stage about the probable orders of magnitude.

The same conclusion applied to the question of whether payment ought to be introduced in Britain on a wider scale. It is feasible and we have indicated the circumstances under which it might be desirable. We have not been able to ascertain whether these circumstances apply currently. It is not for us to decide such things, for only a part of the necessary information consists in data of operations postponed, blood put to no clinical use or less than ideal clinical use, etc. Another set of data is required specifying the social values to be attached to buffer stocks (some of which may never be used clinically), to degrees of risk to the patient, and so on. These decisions are appropriately taken by publicly accountable persons and not by observers or academics whose proper role, at most, is to suggest plausible numbers for their consideration.

Finally there is the ultimate conflict. It may be that in seeking to promote the specific—and moral—end of patients' welfare, we undervalue a greater good: that, in treating giving and selling as means alone, we fail to see that they may also be highly significant ends in themselves.

We do not believe the potential conflict is very real in blood supply. Even if it were, we would recognise that it would be a conflict between ethical ends in which it is by no means obvious that the more general end—preserving 'the gift relationship' in all its manifestations—should dominate the more particular—ensuring adequate blood supplies. In weighing these two, there would be some cost of 'donation only' that would tip the balance in favour of introducing an element of payment. Our principal task has been to demonstrate the feasibility of the payment method and how to mitigate some of its adverse consequences. Its desirability must depend upon the alternative costs at the margin, which remain elusive, and upon society's judgement of the importance to be attached to mutually inconsistent moral objectives.

Appendix

A. Some Geometry of Giving

The elementary economics of giving uses some of the familiar Marshallian geometrical apparatus of demand, which has the virtue of showing the relevance of fairly simple (and traditional) economic analysis in an unusual context as well as suggesting pictorially and rather dramatically where modifications to the usual approach need to be made. It also provides some important interpretations which help both to explain why gifts so frequently take the form they do and to predict some consequences of changing the nature of the relationship between the giver (donor) and the recipient (donee). We shall take it that explaining (evolving a theory consistent with observed behaviour) and predicting (asserting the probable consequences of changing the factors that affect behaviour) are the major functions of social science.

Suppose that one individual, A, makes a gift of a commodity, X, to another individual, B. In Figure I, the individual's Marshallian demand curves[35] are denoted by D^A and D^B. These show for each individual the amount of other goods he is willing to sacrifice for small additions to his ownership of X. A makes a gift of OQ of X to B.[36] This has a market value of OP_mEQ. It is not, we suppose for generality, a free gift since he makes it available at a cost to B of OP_gHQ.[37] The costs and benefits to A and B of the gift can now readily be derived. To do so, as stated in the text, we require to know:

(a) How much the recipient would have spent on X in the absence of the gift.
(b) The cost to the recipient of the gift.
(c) The total value placed by the recipient on the gift.
(d) The total value placed by the recipient on the alternative amount of X he would have bought.
(e) The total value placed by the giver on the gift.
(f) The market value of the gift.

The difference between (a) and (b) (the difference in the recipient's total expenditure on X) is an *effect in cash* which may leave him better or worse off than before

35 'Marshallian' demand curves in the sense that the extent of the gift will not affect the marginal value to anyone of the *numéraire* commodity. The curves have a zero income elasticity. These schedules can therefore be looked at in either of two ways: (a) as showing the amount of X that will be taken at each price, and (b) as showing the marginal value in money of any given amount of X.

36 This does not necessarily imply that A gives *all* his X to B. His marginal valuation curve (demand curve) JE may represent only the relevant part of the schedule for the whole amount of X he has.

37 Many goods or services such as pensions, school meals, health care, council housing, supplied to people under the 'Welfare State' may be regarded, at least in part, as 'gifts' in our sense of the word. We have for convenience assumed that X is finely divisible so that the schedules are continuous. That many gifts in practice are not finely divisible does not affect the substance of the argument.

depending on relative expenditures. In Figure I, this effect is measured by $OP_mKQ_o - OP_gHQ$ (= $P_gP_mKL - Q_oLHQ$).

The difference between (c) and (d) (the difference in the total value of X owned by the recipient) is an *effect in kind* which will leave him better off than before. This effect is measured by $OFGQ - OFKQ_o$ (= Q_oKGQ).

The total gain to the recipient after the gift is measured by the sum of these

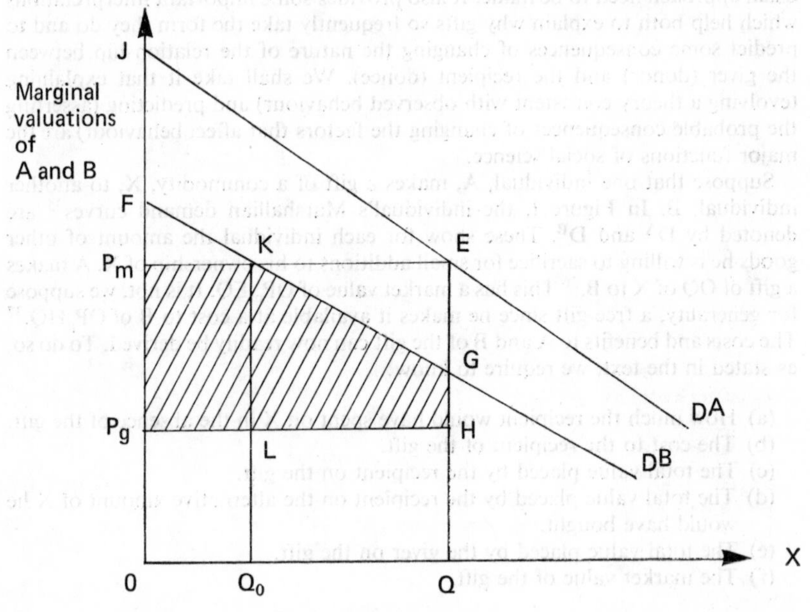

FIGURE I

two differences. This combined effect is measured by the shaded area P_gP_mKGH. It is equivalent to a gain in 'consumers' surplus' from X consumption. By definition, even if the effect in cash is negative, the effect in kind must outweigh it to produce a net benefit to the recipient or he would not accept the gift. The shaded area will therefore be positive and constitutes the recipient's total gain.

The cost to the donor is the difference between (e) and (f) (the total value placed by him on the gift and what he actually paid for it). This is an *effect in kind* representing a loss to the donor of a specific resource. This effect is measured by $OJEQ - OP_mEQ$ (= P_mJE). In addition he loses the difference between (f) and (b) (the market value of the gift less what he gets for it from the recipient). This is measured by $OP_mEQ - OP_gHQ$ (= P_gP_mEH). The total cost to the donor is thus P_gJEH.

Area P_gJEH is the minimal estimate of what the value to him of making the gift is. The donor sacrifices P_gJEH, but the beneficiary receives only P_gP_mKGH. The difference between these two areas appears as a 'waste': P_mJEGK is value of X sacrificed by the donor but not received by the beneficiary. From the point of view of the donor it is not waste since he chooses to make the gift. From the point of view of the beneficiary, however, some of it is waste. For example, if he were permitted to resell his gift at its market value, he would gain additional value in the amount KEG. Alternatively, he would be indifferent between a saleable gift and a money gift equal to OP_mEQ if the gift could be resold at zero transactions cost.

Utility-maximising behaviour implies that the donor will increase the size of his gift (or the frequency of giving) up to the size (or rate) at which the utility loss from increasing the size by a small amount in terms of what is gone without would just be offset by the utility gain from the increase as he sees it. In Figure I, if the donor made the gift available at a subsidised price P_g, the marginal loss of utility from giving up one unit of the gift is measured by the distance EH (EQ if it were given away entirely free of charge). That he gave away more than one unit implies that the increase in utility from giving that unit exceeded the loss of the unit out of his own use of it. In fact, he gave away OQ of X, implying that the marginal valuation of OQ of the gift was equal to the marginal loss of utility P_gJ (OJ if it were entirely free of charge). The important feature of this analysis is that the marginal value of the gift *in his own use* rises as he gives more away (from EH to P_gJ). Conversely, our assumptions imply that the marginal value to

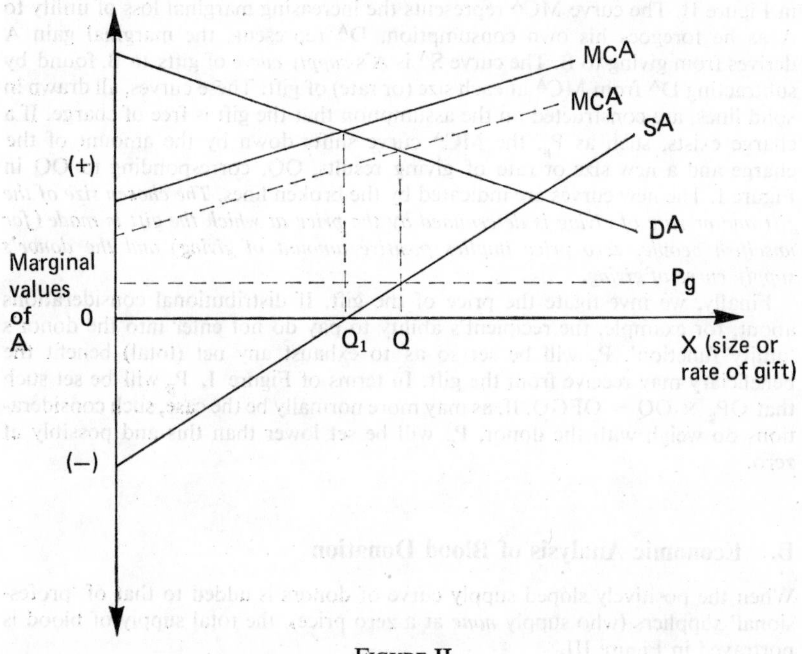

FIGURE II

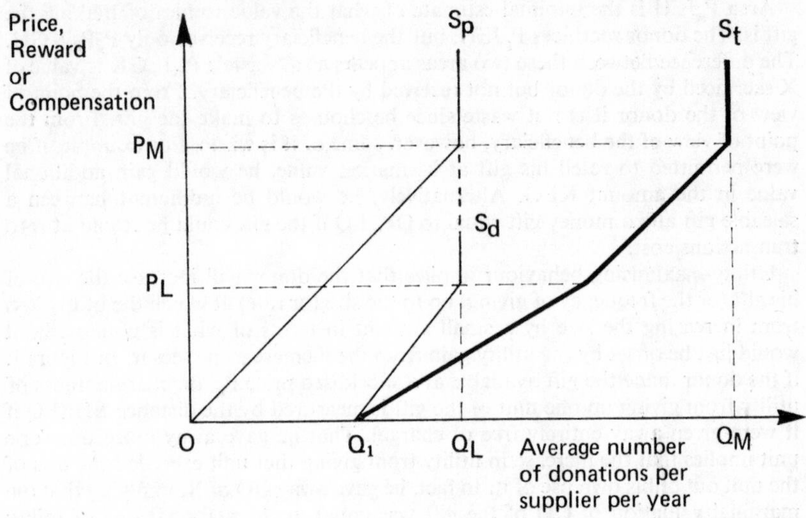

FIGURE III

him of giving *for someone else's use* falls as he gives more away. This is depicted in Figure II. The curve MC^A represents the increasing marginal loss of utility to A as he foregoes his own consumption. D^A represents the marginal gain A derives from giving to B. The curve S^A is A's *supply curve* of gifts to B, found by subtracting D^A from MC^A at each size (or rate) of gift. These curves, all drawn in solid lines, are constructed on the assumption that the gift is free of charge. If a charge exists, such as P_g, the MC^A curve shifts down by the amount of the charge and a new size or rate of giving results, OQ, corresponding to OQ in Figure I. The new curves are indicated by the broken lines. *The chosen size of the gift and/or rate of giving is determined by the price at which the gift is made (for unselfish people, zero price implies positive amount of giving) and the donor's supply curve of giving.*

Finally, we investigate the price of the gift. If distributional considerations about, for example, the recipient's ability to pay do not enter into the donor's 'utility function', P_g will be set so as to exhaust any net (total) benefit the beneficiary may receive from the gift. In terms of Figure I, P_g will be set such that $OP_g \times OQ = OFGQ$. If, as may more normally be the case, such considerations do weigh with the donor, P_g will be set lower than this and possibly at zero.

B. Economic Analysis of Blood Donation

When the positively sloped supply curve of donors is added to that of 'professional' suppliers (who supply *none* at a zero price), the total supply of blood is portrayed in Figure III.

¶ In this Figure, S_d is the supply curve of donors which become sperfectly inelastic only at quantity OQ_L, the limit of the ratе at which they are *permitted* to donate (two donations per year in Britain). S_p is the supply curve of 'professional' suppliers (the less generous members of society) which for any rate of donation requires a higher price than that required for donors, but this curve also becomes perfectly inelastic at the rate of Q_L. (Note, incidentally, that neither of these inelastic sections is based on the behavioural model. Both are due to an institutional rule designed to protect donors' health from excesses of 'generosity' and 'professional suppliers' health from excesses of 'greed'.) S_t, the heavily drawn curve, is the total supply curve which will necessarily become increasingly inelastic at higher prices. These curves, it should be noted, represent the hypothetical qualitative response of *representative* 'professional' donors and suppliers. Thus, OQ_L represents two donations (units) per year, the British standard maximum. OQ_1 represents 1.13 donations, the average number of donations made by civilian blood donors in 1968 at zero price. At a price higher than P_L, further rises will not affect donation since donors already supply the maximum *permitted.* At a price higher than P_M, the maximum rate of supply is already reached. These curves do not, however, depict the total supply to the Blood Transfusion Service for, whereas each donor cannot give more than the maximum permitted (hence producing the vertical parts of the curves), further price rises can be effective in inducing *new suppliers* to present themselves. The total amount of blood supplied per year is thus appropriately represented as in Figure IV.

In Figure IV, S_d represents the supply of donors (who would give blood at zero price) and has a vertical section on the assumption that nothing is done to change the number of persons on the donors' list. S_p is the supply curve of 'professional' donors. S_t is the total supply curve of blood to the system. These curves incorporate, of course, the effect that prices have in encouraging *new* suppliers to enter the system, as well as the effect on *existing* donors and professional suppliers.

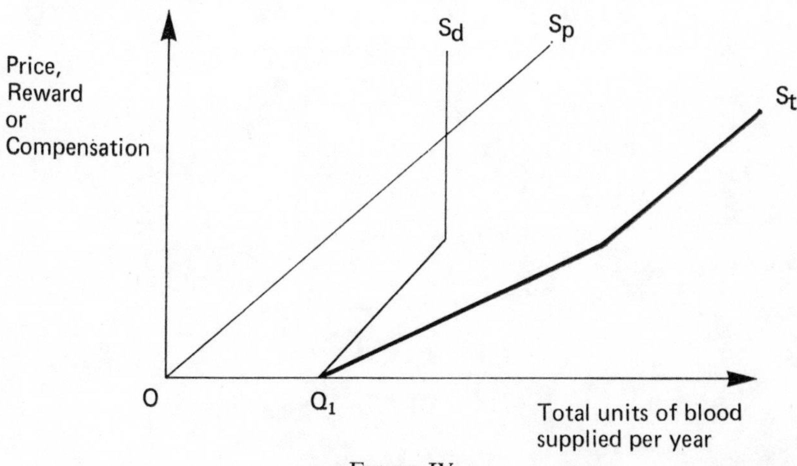

FIGURE IV

2. Blood and American Social Attitudes

THOMAS R. IRELAND

Associate Professor of Economics, University of Missouri—St. Louis

and

JAMES V. KOCH

Chairman, Department of Economics, Illinois State University (Normal, Ill.)

THE AUTHORS

THOMAS R. IRELAND (see Part I, Essay 4, page 64.)

JAMES V. KOCH was born in 1942 and educated at Illinois State University (BA) and Northwestern University (PhD). After spending 1966–67 as a research economist with the Harris Trust and Savings Bank, Chicago, he was appointed Assistant Professor of Economics at the Illinois State University (1967–71). He became Associate Professor of Economics in 1971 and Chairman of the Department of Economics in 1972.

Professor Koch specialises in industrial organisation, micro-economic theory, econometrics-statistics and the economics of education, on which he has written widely in learned journals. His book on *Industrial Organisation and Prices* is to be published shortly by Prentice-Hall.

I. BLOOD AND POLITICS

American society has reached a crisis stage over the sources of blood it uses for medical purposes. Within the past two years, many major American newspapers, notably the *Chicago Tribune*, have devoted considerable space to exposing lurid practices involved in blood buying in so-called 'skid row' areas by unscrupulous commercial blood suppliers.

It has also become a political issue—in part because the late Professor Richard M. Titmuss's *The Gift Relationship*[1] has been read at the top levels of the Government and has reportedly spawned urgent blood research in government bureaus, including the Bureau of Standards. One outcome has been the rumour that tax deductions for blood donations will be proposed by the President in the next session of Congress.

Several academic and government economists who have considered the problem have been unfavourable to Titmuss's[2] conclusions. The ultimate impact of the Titmuss thesis on American policy remains to be seen.

A distorted model

The Gift Relationship is presented as an in-depth comparison of blood supply conditions in the United States and Britain. The US is presented as the model for a private market in blood and Britain as the ideal non-market model, implying an inherent superiority of British over American character and institutions. The tone of the argument is best illustrated by Titmuss's observation that

> 'about 9 per cent [of American blood donations] approximated to the concept of the voluntary community donor who sees his donation as a free gift to strangers in society',[3]

whereas the entire British blood supply approximated to this concept. (In both societies, however, only a small percentage of the population give or sell blood for any reason.) Specifically, Titmuss concluded that

---

[1] Allen and Unwin, 1970.

[2] Simon Rottenberg, 'The Production and Exchange of Used Body Parts', in *Toward Liberty: Essays in honour of Ludwig Von Mises*, vol. II, Institute for Humane Studies, Menlo Park, California, 1972; Kenneth Arrow, 'Gifts and Exchanges', in *Philosophy and Public Affairs*, Summer 1972.

[3] Titmuss, *op. cit.*, p. 95.

'a private market in blood entails much greater risk to the recipient of disease, chronic disability and death . . . is potentially more dangerous to the health of donors . . . [and] produces, in the long run, greater shortages of blood [than a community donor system]'.[4]

One may quibble with the empirical data used to substantiate this argument,[5] but not refute the general argument that the American system, as it now operates, produces more risk of disease to the recipient and quite possibly the donor of a blood transfusion than does the British system. More Americans, on a percentage basis, contract hepatitis from transfusions than Britons (according to Titmuss). What is not valid is his characterisation of the American system as a model for a 'private market' in blood. And there is no truth in the charge that a private market in blood would inherently produce more risk of disease to the recipient or the donor. Nor would it cause a blood shortage.

Ambivalent attitudes

To understand the American system of blood procurement, one must understand the institutional prejudice of Americans against selling blood. Selling blood for money is regarded as 'mercenary' in a sense that receiving other kinds of real benefits for 'giving' blood is not. There is apparently some need for pretence that the primary motivation of the giver is a charitable impulse, but that some recognition may be given in the form of a day off 'to recover' or blood insurance based on the notion that the giver may have 'given' to himself among potential beneficiaries.

In the experiment described below, one of the authors encountered outrage at the mere idea of 'selling' blood for money. Yet rewarding 'gifts' of blood with other kinds of real benefits were received as normal and proper. Obviously, there is an element of the irrational in these attitudes. But in the case of blood, irrationalities abound in many societies—from blood-brother ceremonies of the American Indians to Nazi racism. Without them one cannot understand the American system of blood procurement.[6]

---

4 *Ibid.*, p. 157.

5 Available figures are none too good, but Titmuss's estimate of direct paid donors is probably twice the true figure.

6 This special character of the blood market is discussed in Arrow's paper, *op. cit.*

II. THE US BLOOD MARKET

Dual market structure

The American system of blood provision can best be characterised as a dual market structure. In one part of the market, individuals receive no money payment for blood. Some give for charitable reasons, but a number of non-monetary inducements are used to supplement the charitable impulse in this part of the market, which provides, by Titmuss estimates, two-thirds of the total blood requirements of American hospitals. The true figure may be closer to 80 per cent.[7]

Non-monetary inducements usually take the form of a day off with pay for federal employees, and military personnel may extend their leaves on a one-pint-per-day basis. It is worth noting that the real value to the individual and the real cost to society of 'days off' may be as high as several hundred dollars in the case of high-level federal bureaucrats.

The other form of inducement is blood insurance. Arrangements vary widely in different parts of the United States. The general characteristic is that the donor has 'blood credits' for which he can receive a certain amount of blood when he or his family needs it. A 2 for 1 policy is common: by giving a pint of blood an individual can be said to be purchasing a two-pint blood insurance policy. Since, in some cases, the individual can purchase a similar policy for $10, it can be assumed that this is the approximate value of the policy.[8]

Only about one-seventh of persons who give blood in this non-monetary market receive neither time off nor insurance or some other benefit, which is the source of the 9 per cent figure cited by Titmuss.[9]

The 'monetary' side of the blood market is essentially residual. What is not given free or for non-monetary inducements must be

---

[7] Titmuss, *op. cit.* The latter estimate is derived from a news release of the American Hospital Association dated 8 December, 1971, covering a six-month survey of blood usage by American hospitals.

[8] One insurance policy required the individual to evoke a $10 deposit that could be redeemed if and when a pint of blood was given at a later date.

[9] However, it is difficult to conclude, as Titmuss did, that the charitable motivation is absent simply because a small reward is given. It seems more reasonable to suppose that charitable responses play heavily on donors throughout this part of the market. This is well stated by Arrow, *op. cit.*, pp. 345–6: 'Many of us consider it possible that the process of exchange requires or at least is greatly facilitated by the presence of several . . . virtues. . . . Now virtue may not always be its own reward, but in any case it is not usually bought and paid for at market rates.'

bought. The remaining 20 to 30 per cent of the American blood supply is purchased from individuals who sell their blood at prices from $2 to $35 per pint depending on city and blood type.

Paid blood and the hepatitis risk

Individuals who sell blood for money, as contrasted with other rewards, are much more likely, by a factor estimated upward from 10 to 1, to cause the recipient of a blood transfusion to contract infectious hepatitis. Most types of hepatitis-causing agents (about 75 per cent) cannot be detected in human blood by any presently available test.* Best estimates indicate that the serum which causes hepatitis appears in the blood of mercenary donors in approximately 30 cases per thousand as compared to 3 cases per thousand in non-mercenary donors. It is further estimated that 1 in 150 persons receiving transfusions now contracts hepatitis and that 15 per cent of those over 40 years of age die from it. Total deaths from hepatitis in the United States are estimated from 3,500 to 35,000 per year.[10]

The reasons for the higher incidence of hepatitis among paid donors are related to the environment from which they come. Many commercial blood suppliers acquire blood through store-front outlets in low-income areas, especially those frequented by alcoholics, drug addicts, prostitutes and other individuals unable to maintain a healthy diet. Hepatitis can flourish in such an environment, especially among individuals who are not careful to sterilise hypodermics used for administering heroin 'fixes'. One of the most frequent sources of hepatitis is the transfer of the disease from one individual to another on unclean hypodermics used for administering heroin.

Blood supply—the 'Grants Economy' model

It is from this system of blood procurement that Titmuss reached his conclusions about the potential of a private blood market. In economic terms, however, the American system is not what could properly be called a 'private market for blood', for two reasons. First, many hospitals are not-for-profit institutions and have until recently been exempt from some of the controls a private market would exert over their provision of services. Because hospitals were ultimate suppliers

---

* Recent advances in tests to detect disease-carrying blood are outlined by Dr A. J. Salsbury in the 'Technical Evidence' (below, pp. 179-191).

[10] Constance Holden, 'Blood Banking: Money Is at Root of System's Evils', *Science*, 24 March, 1972.

of blood, patients who contracted hepatitis from transfusions had to try to collect damage compensations from hospitals. Damage suits of this type, until recently, were disallowed by American courts.[11] Hospitals, with no cost incentive to do otherwise, bought and used blood from suspect commercial sources with the excuse that this was the only way they could obtain adequate supplies. Patients were not told of the dangers and blood supplies have not been segregated by source on the ground that no patient would knowingly accept commercial blood if he knew the risks. The hospitals' argument was that each patient had the same risk of contracting hepatitis and that only in this way could enough blood be provided to meet demands.*

Second, and more importantly, a true private market would be characterised by supply offerings in return for money payments. A market in which supply factors have strong elements of charitable motivation rather than profit motivation fits into what Professor Kenneth Boulding has called 'the Grants Economy',[12] in which charitable elements are significant. The supply side of the US blood market is between two-thirds and four-fifths in the Grants Economy and between one-third and one-fifth in the true private sector. The portion of the market which can properly be called private is a residual whose existence is dependent on the *failure of the non-monetary market to provide an adequate supply of blood for the medical requirements of the United States.*

Moreover the system through which the market is divided into Grants Economy and private sectors *requires* that the source of the purely private portion of the market be composed of individuals whose social status is at the bottom of American society, because *the same social attitude which makes the giving of blood for others a virtuous act makes selling blood anathema.* Selling blood is regarded as an act unworthy of a respectable citizen, something which only low-class citizens would do. If this attitude did not exist, it would be hard to imagine that four-fifths of those who give (or trade) blood would be content to do so while the remaining one-fifth receive money payment. That giving blood is virtuous, while selling it is contemptible, is a social institution in the US that Titmuss commended in Britain.

---

[11] This may have changed because of *Cunningham v. MacNeal Memorial Hospital*, 113.111. App. 2nd 74 (1969). The case determined for the first time that a hospital was liable for damages if a patient contracted hepatitis from a transfusion.

* A commentary on the legal implications of recent cases in the US is in the essay by Marilyn J. Ireland in the 'Technical Evidence' (below, pp. 171–178).

[12] *Economics as a Science*, McGraw-Hill, New York, 1970.

III. AN EXPERIMENT

Social institutions can have strange effects on the normal economic forces of supply and demand. A test conducted by one of the authors gives some insight into the way this social attitude to giving and selling blood affects its supply curve. A mass lecture class of principles of economics students, 213 in attendance, were asked to indicate whether or not they would give or sell one pint of blood at various prices. The instructor specified that the question related to giving blood safely, which can be done once each six-week period, and that only one pint could be given or sold at each price by each individual. The results are listed in Table 1.

TABLE 1

dollars/pint	No. of individuals saying they would give one pint
$0.00	59
1.00	41
5.00	65
10.00	109
15.00	132
20.00	145
25.00	161
30.00	163
35.00	163
40.00	165
45.00	165
50.00	170
55.00	170
60.00	170

Giving and selling attitudes demonstrated

There is, of course, an important difference between hypothetical supply curves and individual supply behaviour. (A 'bloodmobile' visited the campus two weeks after the experiment and only seven students, in a check, indicated that they had given blood at a zero price!) What is significant, however, is that 18 individuals listed themselves as *willing* to give blood at a zero price, but not at a price of $1. Independently from their later action, their responses to the questionnaire indicated an institutional difference between a commercial and a partially philanthropic motivation. Further, some of the students chose to use the questionnaire to air their complaint that the professor's whole discussion of the possibility of buying blood was immoral. Thus, while the actual values might not represent points along the supply curve for the class, the general shape of the supply curve is probably indicative of society as a whole (Figure I).

The characteristics of this supply curve are that there is a sharp

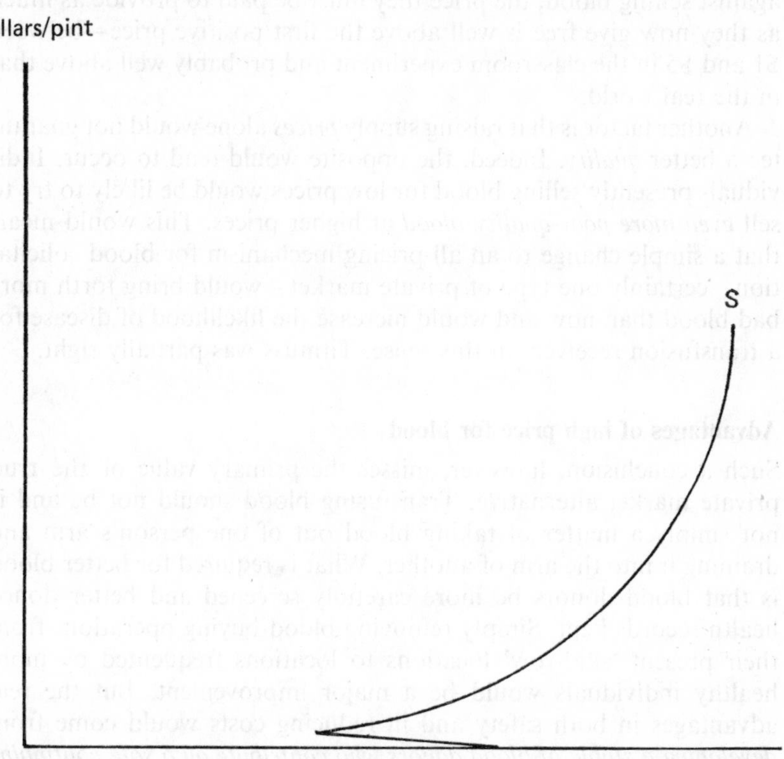

FIGURE I

reduction in the quantity supplied when the offer price is raised from zero to the first positive price. From the first positive price through some unspecified range, the response of suppliers is elastic: small increases in price will bring forth fairly large increases in supply. At some point, however, the supply becomes inelastic, after which large increases in the supply price bring forth only small increases in the quantity supplied.

This supply situation would appear to apply to all elements of the population except those presently in the residual private commercial market. If a move were made to a purely private market for blood, the purpose would be to eliminate present suppliers of dangerous blood and to replace them with individuals of a *healthier background.* Because these healthier individuals have an institutional prejudice against selling blood, the price they must be paid to provide as much as they now give free is well above the first positive price—between $1 and $5 in the classroom experiment and probably well above that in the real world.

Another factor is that raising supply *prices* alone would not guarantee a better *quality*. Indeed, the opposite would tend to occur. Individuals presently selling blood for low prices would be likely to try to sell *even more poor-quality blood* at higher prices. This would mean that a simple change to an all-pricing mechanism for blood solicitation—certainly one type of private market—would bring forth more bad blood than now and would increase the likelihood of disease for a transfusion receiver. In this sense, Titmuss was partially right.

Advantages of high price for blood

Such a conclusion, however, misses the primary value of the true private market alternative. Transfusing blood should not be and is not simply a matter of taking blood out of one person's arm and draining it into the arm of another. What is required for better blood is that blood donors be more carefully screened and better donor health records kept. Simply removing blood-buying operations from their present 'skid-row' locations to locations frequented by more healthy individuals would be a major improvement. But the real advantages in both safety and in reducing costs would come from *developing a stable of blood donors who contribute on a safe continuing basis* and whose medical records are thoroughly checked and cleared to ensure that the individual is healthy and is selling blood at one and only one location.

A price just high enough to attract a sufficient supply of blood to meet American demands would actually be inferior to the present system because poor-risk donors would increase offerings at higher prices. But a price set *high* enough to allow blood buyers to select the *best* from among a surplus of prospective donors coupled with the maintenance of adequate donor records could bring about a significant improvement in quality. Such a system would protect the health of donors as well as recipients, and it certainly would not produce blood shortages, as Titmuss alleged.

Practical possibilities

Showing that a private market could work, however, is a different matter from establishing that it is the only or the best alternative.

The true private market alternative of complete reliance on direct money payments is not the only alternative method of improving the quality of American blood supplies; nor is it the alternative likely to be chosen by American policy-makers. Much more likely, given the realities of bureaucratic big goverment, will be a composite set of actions designed to induce healthy individuals to increase their provision of blood by the 20 to 30 per cent necessary to eliminate the residual private market.

One such action, as mentioned earlier, would be tax deductions from federal personal income tax liabilities for blood donations. They would be equivalent to a government subsidy, but would avoid the mercenary taint of *direct* money payment. Another might be a concerted effort by both government and private leaders to induce more Americans to give blood—an advertising campaign promoting the goodness of blood giving. If extensive enough, it could probably provide at least a short-term solution. Here, however, there would be significant advertising costs as well as the foregone opportunity of promoting some other campaign for the social good. Another measure might involve giving federal employees more indirect payments for blood giving as well as longer leaves for military personnel.

Whether a composite set of inducements would be preferable to a private market would depend on its costs. The issue is not whether a private market *could* work. Of that there should be no question.

3. The US Market in Blood

DAVID B. JOHNSON

Associate Professor of Economics,
Louisiana State University

THE AUTHOR

DAVID B. JOHNSON (see Part I, Essay 5, page 80)

I. BLOOD DONATION IN BRITAIN AND AMERICA

A. General

The late Professor Richard Titmuss, in *The Gift Relationship*, suggested that the British system, in which blood is voluntarily provided, is vastly superior to the American system which, according to Titmuss, relies primarily upon the pricing system. Comparing the US to Britain, he concluded that a private market in blood results in more risk of disease to recipient and donor, increased shortages, a more chaotic system, crass commercialism, creation of a class of blood proletariats, and a decreased quality of life.

Titmuss mentioned the existence of such pervasive externalities in blood donation and transfusion that one suspects he would have classified it as a pure public good (the consumption of which by one individual does not decrease the amount available for consumption by others and from which the individual cannot be excluded). Clearly, blood is *not* a commodity which meets this criterion. Titmuss pointed to externalities that do exist in the provision of blood, primarily in the technical quality of blood arising from the increased incidence of hepatitis occurring among recipients of commercial blood. But many goods exhibit this type of externality. Food, prepared by low-income, 'culturally deprived' groups is more likely to be contaminated than food prepared by highly-paid French chefs and their assistants. The low-income, culturally deprived receive employment as cooks because some individuals prefer to consume lower-quality food at lower prices rather than higher-quality food at higher prices (or no food at all). Blood contamination is not identical to food contamination, but there is no *a priori* reason to assume that the private market cannot make adjustments for the probable contamination of blood as well as for the probable contamination of food.

B. The American System

The American system of blood collection presents an interesting combination of the private and the charity markets. Approximately 8·5 million pints of blood are used annually in the United States,[1] of which one-half comes from the blood centres of the National American Red Cross and the other half is provided by the member banks

[1] *Time*, 11 September, 1972.

of the American Association of Blood Banks (AABB). Less than 5 per cent is provided by commercial blood banks.

The blood banks

The AABB is modelled on the clearing-house mechanism of the US Federal Reserve System. Each AABB district office serves participating blood banks in that district, and the national clearing-house office in San Francisco co-ordinates the programme and settles imbalances between districts. The clearing-house has no direct responsibility for recruiting donors or procuring or processing blood. It functions primarily as a locator of blood and as a bookkeeping agency for the blood banks. A donor in one community who gives a pint of blood for a patient in another community will get his local blood bank to send (or teletype) a credit through the clearing-house system to the blood bank supplying the blood for transfusion. This blood bank, in turn, credits the blood to the patient's account, thereby cancelling the replacement fee which the recipient would otherwise be charged. The clearing-house maintains daily records of each bank's exchanges, balances the accounts at the end of the month, and arranges for the shipments of blood to cancel the net indebtedness among the blood banks.

The AABB is a non-profit, voluntary organisation consisting of approximately 1,400 hospital and community blood banks. It is dominated by the hospital banks, which encourage blood donations by levying a replacement fee (generally in the \$20 to \$50 range) per pint which is returned if the recipient (or other individuals) donate blood to his account.

The Red Cross

The American Red Cross participates in the national clearing-house system, but it also administers its own 59 regional centres. The Red Cross claims that no monetary value should be attached to the blood itself, and charges hospitals only for processing blood (\$8 to \$20 per pint). However, it obtains nearly all its blood through a blood insurance plan which is a proxy for a money payment system. If an individual believes there is a 0·5 probability that he or some member of his family will require a pint costing \$60 in some future time-period, the effective price of his blood donation is \$30.[2]

[2] In order to simplify the discussion it is assumed that the discount rate is zero so that present value equals future value.

With the exception of the procurement of plasma, the commercial blood banks are decreasing in importance. The AABB no longer accepts them as members.

What is a 'volunteer' donor?

Lewis Carroll's Alice and Humpty-Dumpty[3] would have to engage in a prolonged dialogue if they were to analyse the meaning of the word 'voluntary' as used by Americans for blood procurement. Officials of AABB and the Red Cross and others state that their organisations rely upon 'volunteer' donors, who are essential for a sufficient, healthy, and flexible system of blood supply. They criticise the operations and the existence of the commercial blood firms which pay the donors for the blood they provide. For some reason, these officials refuse to recognise that a price paid *ex ante* (Red Cross), or a price paid *ex post* (AABB member hospitals), is nevertheless a price.[4,5] However, the American system is not as price-oriented as

[3] *Through the Looking Glass*, Chapter VI.

[4] There are a number of bills pending in Congress which would provide a tax incentive for individuals to donate blood. One bill, HR 853, provides that an individual may credit as a charitable contribution (deductible from income) $25 for every pint of blood donated within a year, with total allowable deductions equal to $125. This scheme would favour the high-income groups because a decrease in their income of $25 results in a larger tax saving than a $25 decrease in the income of lower-income groups. Another bill would establish a national blood bank scheme under the supervision of a director appointed by the Secretary of Health, Education and Welfare.

[5] In the 13 August, 1971, edition of *Science*, William Bevan wrote an editorial mentioning Professor Titmuss's book but approving the tax plan described in footnote 4. Richard H. Aster of the Milwaukee Blood Center criticised the editorial support of the tax credit in a letter to the editor which appeared in the 28 January, 1972, issue:

'In his editorial "On Stimulating the gift of blood" (13 August, p. 583), William Bevan supports H.R. 853, a bill to award a $25 federal income-tax deduction for "voluntary" blood donation. Not only could this bill cost the American taxpayers $30 to $40 million annually, but there is no certainty that it would accomplish its goal of increasing the quality and quantity of blood that is used in transfusion. A more basic question may also be raised. Is it right and necessary to convert most of our blood-donor population into one of *de facto* paid donors by legislative means?

'The answer depends, as Bevan notes, on one's "faith in the altruistic principle". The principle appears not to work in the Soviet Union, where blood donation is rewarded by lavish government subsidies, but it is operative in England, Australia, and New Zealand, where voluntary donors supply 100 per cent of the blood needs. That it can also work in the United States is shown by the successful operation of all-voluntary blood-donation systems in Seattle, Milwaukee, and other communities. Especially noteworthy is the success recently achieved in the recruitment of voluntary donors in New York City through the efforts of the Community Blood Council of Greater New York, which now supplies 50 per cent of the blood needs of that area.

'Possibly H.R. 853 is needed to prod the American public into making the gift of blood that is so essential to the well-being of their less fortunate fellows and costs them

Titmuss suggested. It comprises an interesting combination of the private and charity markets. A major portion of the blood obtained by the Red Cross is the result of arrangements made with an employer or union whereby *all* employees or members are insured for blood requirements during a period if a stated *percentage* of their employees or members will donate blood during that period.

In one sense, these plans are similar to a private market transaction in which a group is buying an insurance plan and paying for it in kind. In another sense, they are part of the charity market because firms and unions often use social pressures to induce individual members to contribute. Whether intended or not, this scheme is an effective way of sub-dividing the population into smaller groups in which social pressures can be applied more effectively.

The charges by Titmuss that the American system of procuring and allocating blood is characterised by shortages, by more evidence of hepatitis, and by general chaos, even if factually correct, do not constitute proof of pricing failures. There are few reliable statistics on the 'shortage' of blood in the US, but if they exist they might be caused by sudden increases in demand resulting from new surgical techniques, population mobility, the Vietnam War, spatial concentrations of large blood users, and the cultural and social heterogeneity of the American population.

---

only a few minutes of their time with slight physical discomfort. Even larger subsidies may be necessary to obtain kidneys, skin, and other tissues for the rapidly increasing demands of organ transplantation. On the other hand, cynicism and materialism may be less rampant than we are sometimes led to believe. Spared from legislation such as H.R. 853, perhaps we can yet follow the English example.'

Because Mr Aster is associated with the Milwaukee Blood Center, which he claims to have a 'successful operation of *all-voluntary* blood-donation system', a letter of inquiry was sent to the Milwaukee Blood Center and was answered by Mr Timm Hurst, Administrator. The questions and answers were:

(1) What was the total quantity of blood donated during 1971? *Answer*: 66,233 pints.

(2) What percentage of this blood was donated under a blood assurance plan in which donors receive credit for their donated blood in event of a future need of blood by themselves or members of their families? *Answer*: 73 per cent including 6 per cent for the (AABB) clearing-house.

(3) What percentage of this blood was donated as replacement blood for themselves, friends or relatives? *Answer*: 26 per cent.

(4) What percentage was donated because of a price payment for blood? *Answer*: 1 per cent.

(5) What percentage was donated that has not been classified above? *Answer*: Zero per cent.

Needless to say, this is *not* an 'all-voluntary' system.

Diverse system of supply, not 'chaos'

American blood supply may have appeared chaotic to Titmuss because, in contrast to the British system in which the channels of collection and distribution are a state monopoly and the customer is a monopsonistic client, the American experience is a combination of local, regional, and national Red Cross units; private, charitable, and government hospitals; commercial blood firms; and a private clearing-house. The existence of multiple entities of suppliers, intermediaries, and demanders does not imply 'chaos', any more than the existence of numerous individual entities in the market-place signifies confusion.

Although the provision and allocation of blood in the US is more price-oriented than in Britain, a number of impediments constrain the market system from functioning effectively. *First*, pressures to eliminate 'blood commercialism' emanating from the Red Cross, the AABB, and the bad press resulting from Congressional committees and the communications media have limited entry of firms. *Second*, most hospitals are non-competitive and not profit-oriented, and thus do not have the incentive to economise. Under current institutional arrangements, hospitals do not have sufficient incentive to develop sophisticated estimation techniques and inventory controls. In addition, the Red Cross, which provides the major portion of blood to hospitals, does not charge for it. *Third*, the implied warranty law which applies to most products is not applicable in 27 states because their legislatures have intentionally defined blood as a service instead of a product, thus exempting blood from implied warranty. If the warranty law did apply, the procurers of blood and the hospitals would be induced to take precautions which other private market firms must take. It is the political, not the private, market that should be blamed for this failure.*

Hepatitis risk and incentives

Titmuss's claim of increased incidence of hepatitis among recipients of commercial blood in the US was an apparently factual statement, but there is no reason to relate the deficiency to the pricing system. The non-profit hospitals have generally not had the incentive to pay higher prices for higher-quality blood and to invest in systems of quality and inventory control. The problem may lie not in the price

* Further commentary on the legal aspects of blood supply in the US is in the essay by Marilyn J. Ireland, in the 'Technical Evidence' below, pp. 171–178.

system but in the *non*-market institutions which have produced ignorance and an unwillingness by users to pay for good-quality blood.

II. THE PRICING OF BLOOD

Titmuss observed that total blood donations fell when a pricing system was inaugurated, which led him to conclude that fewer units of blood would be supplied by a blood pricing system in Britain than by the current voluntary system. Assuming his observations were correct, his general conclusion does not necessarily follow. One can easily understand why total quantity supplied may decrease as the system is changed from zero to, say, $5 per pint. This relatively low price may attract individuals from the 'lower classes' whose opportunity costs are relatively low, and other individuals previously volunteering their blood may not want to be associated or identified with 'lower class' blood suppliers, or they may dislike giving blood when other are being paid. Whatever their reasons, some of the former volunteers may stop supplying blood when pricing is introduced, and the price may not be high enough to induce an offsetting increase in paid donors. The total quantity and quality of blood supplies will therefore decrease. There is however *some* price at which both the quantity and the quality problems would be solved. If the price were raised to $50 per pint, the quantity supplied would probably exceed volunteer donations. And individuals from higher income- and class-groups would be attracted so that the general *quality* of blood should improve. If the incidence of hepatitis is higher among individuals from lower income, social, geographical, or educational classes, they could be excluded from participation by more sophisticated detection and reporting procedures.

A positive price paid to a supplier of a good is not sufficient evidence to eliminate an altruistic motivation.* An altruistically-motivated blood donor may be willing to provide blood at a price *lower* than the inconvenience costs to him but not at a *zero* price. Hence, a positive price is not incompatible with altruism. Conversely, the *absence* of a positive price paid to blood suppliers, as in the British NHS, is not sufficient evidence of altruism. Titmuss ignored the potential existence of social pressure which may stimulate these 'volunteer' activities.

* David B. Johnson, 'The Charity Market', in Part I, Essay 5, especially pp. 88–90.

Are British blood transfers regressive?

Titmuss's major contribution was the extensive accumulation of data. His book constitutes the best source of information on the blood system in the US, and probably in Britain as well, although his use of selective quotes and episodes prejudges the argument. One of his most interesting sets of statistics was the result of a survey conducted on the characteristics of blood donors in the Birmingham, Manchester, and South-East Metropolitan hospital districts.

Table 29 in *The Gift Relationship*[6] gives the percentage distribution of donors among income classes, which Titmuss claimed was 'broadly representative of the general eligible population'. Tables 13 and 15,[7] however, suggest that the higher social (and presumably income) classes receive more than their proportionate quantity of blood transfusions. Titmuss showed surprise at these results:

> 'we would have expected—particularly under a free National Health Service—to find that, taking account of these factors, blood transfusions would be relatively more numerous among the [lower classes]'. (p. 136)

Since blood donors represented the approximate proportionality of various social and income classes in the general population,[8] but the higher-income classes received a more than proportionate quantity of blood transfers, there seems to be a net redistribution of blood from the poor to the rich. If payments were made for blood, as in the US, there would be a redistribution from the rich to the poor. The US, in terms of blood incidence, is clearly more progressive in structure than Britain. It is a perplexing situation, in which Titmuss preferred a British *regressive* system to an American *progressive* one.[9]

---

[6] *Op. cit.*, p. 292: 'Percentage distribution of income per week before tax of chief earner in all donor families by sex and for employees in FES, 1966.'

[7] Table 13: 'Percentage of donors in each sex, social class and number of donations group who had received a blood transfusion' (p. 138). Table 15: 'Percentage of all donors by social class in whose immediate family at least one member has received blood' (p. 139).

[8] Because 75 per cent of the donors in Titmuss's sample were drawn from the relatively more prosperous areas of Birmingham and the South-East Metropolitan district, the number of donors in the higher income (and social) groups may have been over-represented. On the basis of the data provided by this non-random sample, it is reasonable to conclude that individuals in the higher-income groups may contribute blood in a proportion less than their relative proportion in the population of Britain.

[9] Due to the partial commercialisation of the blood system in the US it is probably slightly progressive. The statistical evidence on charitable contributions in the US suggests a degree of regressiveness which further indicates that replacing a private market system with a charity market system will produce a more regressive structure. (Appendix to my essay in Part I, Table 7, p. 106.)

Objective evidence lacking

Titmuss avoided quotes, studies, or episodes that would suggest that any quantity or quality problems exist in the British blood system, while quoting many adverse statements about the American system. Such non-randomness destroys the objectivity, though not necessarily the validity, of his conclusions. Additionally, results obtained from questionnaires on motivations for some action are not likely to yield the truth, especially when the letter sent to the donors stated that the purpose of the survey was to find out more about the characteristics of people 'who perform such a vital humanitarian service by giving blood voluntarily to the National Blood Transfusion Service' (p. 123). One doubts whether Diogenes's search would have terminated had he happened upon those individuals who completed these unaudited questionnaires.

Conclusion

Any commodity, including blood, may be provided and allocated through a number of institutional mechanisms:

(a) a system whereby each qualified citizen could be required to contribute a pint of blood every X months—the Israelis and the Swiss use this procedure to man their armies, and the Chinese, according to news reports, to remove snow from streets and walk-ways;
(b) a lottery system in which individuals are selected to provide the good, such as in the current US military draft system;
(c) the queuing system, as in some parts of the British Health Service and in American football games;
(d) the pure charity market, or gift relationship, in which individuals voluntarily contribute goods below the market price to people they believe are in need, or to an agency which, in turn, makes the allocative decisions;
(e) the pricing mechanism in a purely private market or in combination with the political or charity markets.

If individuals in Britain freely contribute blood without fear of social, financial, or political pressure, *if* the resulting supply is sufficient to provide all the blood demanded at zero price, and *if* resources are not employed in advertisements, progaganda, etc., to convince people they should contribute, blood is no longer an economic good. Although the evidence clearly contradicts these assumptions, such a system would truly be preferable to all others and, while we in the US may not be able to duplicate the British system because of differing size, heterogeneity, mobility of population, traditions, etc., we would have to conclude that the British would be a remarkable people indeed.

Technical Evidence

A. The Legal Framework of the Market for Blood

MARILYN J. IRELAND

Assistant Professor of Law, Washington University School of Law, St. Louis, Missouri

THE AUTHOR

Ms. Marilyn J. Ireland received her JD degree from the University of Chicago Law School in 1969 (where she was a member of the editorial board of the *University of Chicago Law Review*). After practising with a large Chicago law firm, she joined the faculty of the Washington University School of Law, where she is now Assistant Professor of Law and Associate Dean of the School.

Ms. Ireland is married to Professor Thomas R. Ireland; they have two children.

I. INTRODUCTION

The social goal of an 'adequate' supply of high-quality blood for transfusions has been submerged by social thinking and legal institutions more concerned with motives than with results. In the United States this confusion has led to a high incidence of infectious hepatitis contracted through blood transfusions.[1] Only recently, in the state of Illinois, have the courts departed from a series of unworkable legal principles that exculpated blood donors and suppliers from any liability for damage inflicted upon transfusion patients due to poor quality blood. By emphasising intentions rather than results, the courts abdicated their responsibility to give quality guidance in the medical market-place for blood.

It is not difficult to trace to its source the unfortunate emphasis of American courts on the charitable motives of volunteer donors and hospitals. Good thoughts, high intentions, and a noble state of mind too often dominate our thinking. This preoccupation with state of mind frequently obscures the consequences of a given action or rule. An 'adequate' supply of wholesome human blood is essential for the practice of modern medicine on which civilised men now rely. Procurement institutions and the laws which govern them should be directed toward achieving this goal.

Blood for transfusions is procured in the United States from a variety of sources, handled by a variety of middlemen blood banks, and dispensed by a variety of hospitals, clinics, and physicians. Some blood is obtained from voluntary donors, others from paid donors. Blood banks may be run by non-profit charities, or by commercial, profit-making enterprises. The hospitals and clinics dispensing the blood, in the form of transfusion, may be religiously affiliated, charitable, or profit-making. Commentators on this system have frequently abhored the commercial, profit-oriented, paid donor aspects of this system. American courts have simply ignored them.

In abhoring and ignoring the non-charitable market for blood, both the commentators and courts are guilty of emphasising motives rather than results. For example, Titmuss praises voluntary blood donor systems because the donors have spiritually advanced themselves.

'. . . in terms of the free gift of blood to unnamed strangers there is no formal contract, no legal bond, no situation of power, domination, constraint or compulsion, no sense of shame or guilt, no gratitude imperative, no need for penitence, no money and no explicit guarantee of or wish for a reward or a return gift. They are acts of free will; of the exercise of choice; of conscience without shame.'[2]

---

[1] E.g., Medical Note: 'Sweating Blood', *Time*, 19 October, 1970. Hepatitis is one of the most troublesome of contaminants of whole blood because of the difficulty in detecting its presence.

[2] *The Gift Relationship*, *op. cit.*, p. 89. The 'good thoughts' analysis appears particu-

As Titmuss himself recognised, there is no room for *responsibility*, which he characterised as doctor-patient 'hostility', in such a system.[3]

II. CHARITABLE IMMUNITY

Under an ancient common law doctrine, charitable institutions have a limited immunity from liability. Charities could not be held responsible for injury caused by their negligence. Negligence, an 'evil' state of mind sufficient for liability in most cases, was cancelled out by charitable motives. Judges rationalised this rule by noting that charities could not pay the penalties or costs of a judgement without re-allocating moneys which otherwise would be devoted to charitable purposes.[4]

Because most American hospitals are non-profit, the charitable immunity doctrine resulted in abandoning unfortunate patients, who contracted hepatitis through transfusion. Another legal doctrine, privity, transferred the hospitals' immunity to earlier links in the blood procurement chain.[5] Blood banks and donors thus 'inherited' the immunity of a charitable successor in the chain, even if they themselves were profit-oriented. Put simply, the injured patient was totally without remedy.

Economic effects of immunity

In applying the charitable immunity doctrine to the blood procurement and dispensing system, the American courts not only failed to examine remote participants; they also failed to consider the consequences of applying the charitable immunity doctrine to the blood market. By failing to assess legal responsibility, the courts removed the normal financial incentives to improve quality. This proved particularly disastrous in blood procured through profit-oriented institutions.[6] In addition, the 'feed-back'

---

larly appealing in relation to blood procurement problems. This may result from a deep-seated emotional antipathy to vampirism. Blood also has important human and even religious connotations to many people. These non-rational responses can only be overcome by turning the medical act of transfusion into a religious, or at least charitable, occasion.

[3] *Ibid*., p. 170, also Ch. 9 generally.

[4] 'The charitable immunity doctrine created an impossible morass of law, with which lawyers and judges could not hope to cope. The doctrine was applied unevenly from circumstance to circumstance and from state to state. It was also riddled with exceptions that had little to recommend them and unduly complicated legal proceedings. One general compendium of the laws of the various states, *Corpus Juris Secundum*, devotes 12 pages to this narrow doctrine. The complexity and length of this text is witness to the fact that the doctrine of charitable immunity defies rational simplification, in the form of an overview, normally available from a legal encyclopedia.' (14 *CJS* §75, pp. 544–556, 1939.)

[5] The doctrine of privity, where applicable, prevents a remote purchaser from suing the original seller. A purchaser may hold accountable only the person with whom he dealt directly.

[6] Task Force Report of *Chicago Tribune* reporters, published in series beginning 12 September 1971.

of information which results from legal liability could not operate. Profit-oriented and non-profit blood procurement agencies alike were hampered in their quality control by inadequate information.

Judicial abnegation had an immediate adverse impact on commercial blood banks and paid donor systems. These profit-oriented systems operate like any other free enterprise market, providing the quality and quantity demanded by the society in which they exist. Some commentators on blood procurement improperly assume that paid donor and commercial blood bank systems necessarily result in poor quality. The poor quality of some commercial blood markets observed by such authors results not from the fact that the blood is procured from paid donors, but from the metaphysical approach to blood procurement they themselves advocate.

A good legal system assists the operation of the free market when it places legal responsibility for defective goods upon the person who can control and minimise such defects. One important goal is the proper allocation of risks. Not all risks are unavoidable. By placing legal liability upon the person best able to prevent future recurrences of injury, the courts perform the function not only of assessing blame, but more importantly of reducing the number of similar losses in the future.[7] The commercial blood bank that collects low-quality blood from a highly infected sector of the public, for example, must be held accountable for the damage it causes. Freed of legal responsibility by the 'charitable immunity' doctrine of early American law, the market for commercial blood in the US predictably became anarchic, specialising in low-quality, low-cost blood.

The information effect of judical abnegation reduced the quality of blood from profit and non-profit blood procurement agencies alike. Legal responsibility does more than simply fix blame. It offers a system of information feed-back to the person held responsible. A blood bank or donor held accountable for injury to a patient is told that a particular pint of blood caused in a particular patient a particular ill-effect, with ascertained costs. This information is seldom determined when the victim suffers in silence, realising his legal impotence.

Fortunately, the charitable immunity doctrine gradually fell out of favour in US Courts. Unfortunately, the blood procurement system was not a beneficiary of this change. Courts rapidly and surprisingly ruled that blood is a service, not a product.[8]

The service of blood transfusions

Does a patient in need of blood receive a service, the service of placing a needle in his arm through which passes blood plasma? Or does he receive

[7] Blum and Kalven, *Public Law Perspectives on a Private Law Problem*, Little Brown & Co., 1965.

[8] E.g., *Perlmutter v. Beth David Hospital*, 308 N.Y. 100, 123 N.E.2d 792 (1954).

a product—blood? As statements of fact, it would be difficult to argue with either view. Both a service and a product are involved. But the judicial conclusion to focus on the immediate service of transfusion rather than the underlying product had serious legal consequences. It was not enough for a patient to show that the particular pint of blood he received was defective. He had to show in addition that the physician or hospital was negligent in performing the transfusion service.

This narrow view of courts in focussing on the immediate decision of a physician whether or not to transfuse once again resulted in immunity to blood-procuring agencies. A physician might well be exercising reasonable judgement in deciding to transfuse a critically ill patient, even if some portion of the blood supplied to him by a blood bank is tainted. Such a calculated risk is often justified. Nonetheless, in focussing on this immediate calculation of the physician, the courts did not provide blood-procuring agencies with guidance or incentive to improve quality. The quality of blood available to the physician was taken as a given and immutable fact.

III. THE ILLINOIS JUDICIAL REVOLUTION

Very recently the judiciary of one state, Illinois, finally undertook to provide for the market for blood the same legal guidance provided for other product markets. In 1970 the Illinois Supreme Court looked beyond the immediate act of transfusion to the entire blood procurement system and concluded that blood was, indeed, a product.[9] This court then applied to blood the newly emerging doctrine of strict product liability. In practice, this means that whenever a patient contracts hepatitis from a transfusion given in Illinois, the hospital will be required to pay damages to the patient. The hospital may, in turn, pass on this liability to its outside source of supply.

Beneficial results

The predictable result of this change has occurred. Hospitals have begun careful monitoring of their sources of whole blood. Blood banks, commercial and non-profit, have improved their handling to decrease spoilage and mixing. Commercial and non-profit blood banks have also begun to improve the quality of acceptable donors.

---

[9] *Cunningham v. MacNeal Mem. Hosp.*, 266 N.E.2d 897 (1970). The Illinois approach has been adopted in whole or in part by Washington, Florida, Pennsylvania and New Jersey. *Reilly v. King County Cent. Blood Bank, Inc.*, 492 P. 2d 246 (Wash. App. 1971); Mod. 1971 Sess. L. Ch. 56 para. 1 (Wash.); *Russell v. Community Blood Bank, Inc.*, 185 So. 2d 749 (Fla. Appl. 1966), aff'd. in part 196 So. 2d 115 (Fla. 1967), holding blood banks but not hospitals liable; *Hoffman v. Misericordia Hospital*, 439 Penn. 501, 267 A. 2d 867 (1970), using a warrantee approach; *Jackson v. Muhlenberg Hospital*, 96 N.J. Super. 314; 232 A.2d 879 (L. Div. 1967), recognising warrantee disclaimer. See also *Gottsdanker v. Cutler Labs*, 182 Cal. App. 2d 602, 6 Cal. Rptr. 320 (1960).

The Illinois approach will result in a decrease in the risk of hepatitis to patients. It will increase the quality of blood by supplying information on the sources of defective blood. It will also supply financial incentives, in the form of fewer adverse judgements, to those hospitals and blood banks which supply quality blood.

The Illinois approach will result in better blood quality in both the commercial and non-commercial blood markets. However, the largest improvement will probably occur in the more responsive commercial market. The increased information on desirable blood sources can be used only to a limited extent by agencies that rely on a strictly limited number of volunteer donors. No such limitation exists on the larger population of potential paid donors. Similarly, cost incentives arising from adverse judgements will operate more efficiently in the commercial market which is directly oriented to profit.

One desirable effect of the Illinois approach can hardly be denied. It will decrease the spread of hepatitis. Critics of the decision complain, however, that this benefit will not be costless. They cite scarcity and higher costs as disadvantages to the new product liability approach.

Inadequate blood supplies for needed transfusions would, indeed, be an unfortunate result from attempts to improve the quality of blood. Important surgical procedures would have to be postponed or cancelled. Patients would die from anaemia rather than hepatitis. The fear of scarcity is not justified, however, because of the mixed commercial/non-commercial nature of the American blood procurement system. To be sure, the supply of *volunteer* blood is strictly limited. Rejection of high-risk donors will therefore result in a smaller total supply of blood. The supply of *paid donor* blood is not subject to such rigorous quantity limitations. The quantity of blood lost by rejection of low-risk donors can be counterbalanced simply by purchasing requirements from other potential donors at the market price. Should the demand for good-quality blood result in decreased volunteer suppliers, this deficiency can be compensated by purchasing more blood from paid donors. Commercial blood banks can be expected to respond to the quantity and quality demands of the market when guided by appropriate rules of legal responsibility.

Effects of higher quality

Quality, of course, usually costs more. Critics may therefore be correct in urging that the Illinois decision will result in a higher per-pint price for blood. Because most patients carry health insurance, this price increase will usually be borne in the first instance by insurance companies. If this increased per unit cost is not offset by other cost savings, it will eventually result in an increase in insurance premiums and a decrease in the profits of insurance companies.[10] However, the increased per-unit cost of higher-

[10] The demand elasticity for medical insurance will determine the extent to which

quality blood will be offset, at least in part, by the savings inherent in blood quality improvement.

Higher-quality blood purchased at a higher per-pint price will infect fewer patients. The total medical expenses of transfusion victims, as a class, will therefore decline. Money spent on quality blood for transfusions will also decrease the loss of income, crippling and death caused by hepatitis.

All these savings will be realised not only by the patients, but also by their insurance companies. Fewer hepatitis sufferers means fewer hospital days paid for by health insurance companies. Similarly, insurance companies will be faced with fewer demands for benefits under income protection and death benefit plans.

The net cost of higher-priced quality blood to insurance companies cannot easily be calculated. It is certainly not measured simply by the per-unit cost of blood. Indeed, the savings may more than offset increased per-unit costs. It would not be surprising if fewer infected patients reduced insurance costs.

If critics of the Illinois approach are correct, the price of medical insurance will increase. The rate increase would purchase an otherwise difficult to find form of life and disability insurance. The additional premium will purchase an actual decrease in the possibility of medical misfortune instead of merely paying the insured after disaster strikes.

IV. SUMMARY

Illinois and other states following its lead have chosen to purchase higher-quality blood. This quality improvement is brought about by a legal rule which assesses hospitals and blood banks whenever they infect a patient with poor-quality blood. This assessment of liability gives information on the source of defective blood. It also gives a financial incentive to these institutions to improve the quality of blood.

The information and incentive provided by the Illinois view of legal responsibility will operate most effectively upon commercial and paid donor systems. The financial incentive to improve quality will directly influence commercial blood banks because they are guided by the profit motive.

The increase in the quality of blood can be accomplished in the US without creating a shortage. Any decrease in volunteer supplies can be offset through the paid donor system.

Higher-quality blood will probably result in higher per unit blood prices. However, this increased price will be offset, in part or in whole, by a decrease in the infection, disability, and death of transfusion recipients. Quality is not always a bad investment.

---

insurance companies can pass on increased costs to policy-holders in the form of higher premiums. For a discussion of the application of elasticity to the allocation of increased costs to middlemen, Richard A. Musgrave, *The Theory of Public Finance*, McGraw-Hill, New York, 1959, pp. 276–87 (he discusses increased cost in the form of a tax on profits).

B. Medical Evidence: Blood Donation and the Australia Antigen

A. J. SALSBURY, MA, MD
Consultant Haematologist, Brompton Hospital, London

THE AUTHOR

DR A. J. SALSBURY received his medical education at Jesus College, Cambridge and St Bartholomew's Hospital. After a period as Senior Lecturer in Haematology at St Bartholomew's Hospital, he is now Consultant Haematologist and Clinical Tutor at Brompton Hospital, Honorary Consultant at the Royal Marsden Hospital and Vice-Dean of the Cardiothoracic Institute.

I. BLOOD DEMAND AND SUPPLY

The United Kingdom is fortunate in having a highly efficient transfusion service, which is able to satisfy most of the present demand for blood. The National Blood Transfusion Service has steadily increased in recent years, both in its number of donors and in the amount of blood donated, as the Table shows:

	Annual rate of increase of donors[1]	*Annual rate of increase of blood donations*[2]
	%	%
1961	8·6	5
1962	5·2	4
1963	5·4	4
1964	3·0	6
1965	3·0	5
1966	8·0	6
1967	5·6	3
1968	2·9	2

[1] Figures for 1961 to 1966 quoted from Cooper and Culyer (footnote 1); for 1967–1968 calculated from Titmuss (footnote 2).

[2] Calculated from figures supplied in Titmuss.

At the same time, there is a very markedly increasing demand for blood and blood products. This is due to new medical developments and also to changing social circumstances, such as the bigger and bloodier accidents resulting from more cars and faster roads.

New operations raise demand for blood

The most significant medical advances contributing to an increased demand for blood are:

1. The development of more ambitious operations. They include much more extensive operations for the removal of cancer than was once thought feasible, and operations on the heart. The latter often use a 'by-pass' technique, with an external machine taking over the functions of the heart and lungs. The machine needs to be 'primed' with blood: eight or twelve pints of blood are commonly used. Although heart transplants are at present in disfavour, liver, kidney and occasional lung transplants still take place. It is probable that, in the near future, transplantation of the entire thoracic contents, i.e. heart, lungs and great vessels, will be performed.

---

[1] M. H. Cooper and A. J. Culyer, *The Price of Blood*, Hobart, Paper 41, Institute of Economic Affairs, London, 1968.

[2] R. M. Titmuss, *The Gift Relationship*, Allen and Unwin, London, 1970.

2. The rapidly increasing use of renal dialysis machines for patients with kidney failure. These instruments also have to be 'primed' with blood. It has been estimated that less than 30 per cent of patients requiring treatment in the UK have a chance of receiving it.[3] The limitation is largely due to current shortage of staff and money but, if these problems were solved, the extra demand for blood would be considerable.

3. Many patients with blood diseases once thought untreatable are now being kept alive for longer and longer periods. The classic example is haemophilia, but patients with leukaemia and aplastic anaemia, although rarely completely cured, can be maintained, often for some years, in reasonably good health. Regular and multiple transfusions of blood or blood products are essential for treatment. Thus, over the years, one patient receives a very large quantity of blood from many donors.

Methods of increasing supply

It is very difficult to see how this increasing demand is to be met. The rate of increase of the National Blood Transfusion Service is steady, but slow. It is of the utmost importance to develop new ways of increasing blood supplies.

There are two means by which more blood can be made available. One is to reduce the wastage of blood, the other to increase the number of donations of blood. Wastage of blood is relatively low in this country, but could be lowered further. Some waste occurs because blood cannot be stored indefinitely and goes 'out of date' if not used within three weeks. Although such blood can be used to make blood products, its main component, red blood cells, is lost. It is possible that improved methods of blood storage may lengthen the time before blood goes 'out of date'.

It is also feasible to increase the numbers of patients deriving benefit from a single unit of blood by separating the blood into its constituent parts. For example, one bottle could be split into packed red blood cells for the treatment of blood loss, a platelet concentrate for the treatment of bleeding due to shortage of platelets, and into cryoprecipitate for the treatment of disorders such as haemophilia. However, many of these preparations have to be given within a few hours of separation.

Another cause of wastage is unnecessary transfusions, often in amounts too small to benefit the patient. For example, there is a belief among some surgeons that 'topping up' a patient with a pint of blood is beneficial: this is not so. It has been estimated that the use of blood was unnecessary in 6·5 per cent of all transfusions.[4] Many pre-operative transfusions could be avoided if a patient were tested for anaemia when first considered for

---

[3] D. N. S. Kerr, *Proc. Roy. Soc. Med.*, 60, 1967, p. 1,195.

[4] C. W. Graham-Stewart, *Lancet*, *ii*, 1960, p. 421.

operation and treated appropriately.[5] Such pre-operative testing has yet to become a universal routine. However, even if wastage could be reduced, it is unlikely that enough blood would be saved to cover all future demands.

The second solution—to increase blood donations—will be considered later (p. 190). At this stage, it is pertinent to examine a new development which has a direct bearing on the question: the discovery of the Australia antigen.

II. THE AUSTRALIA ANTIGEN

Serum hepatitis

The severest hazard in blood transfusion is the risk of serum hepatitis developing in the recipient. It is an unpleasant disease causing acute inflammation of the liver. It often leads to protracted sickness and carries a definite mortality risk. The disease may be transmitted by any procedure in which the skin or mucous membranes are punctured by instruments which have become contaminated with the blood of a carrier of the disease,[6] or, of course, by transfusion of blood from a carrier. It is caused by a virus called B, to distinguish it from virus A, which causes infective hepatitis. Infective hepatitis is a disease similar to serum hepatitis but transmitted by contact and, on the whole, has a shorter incubation period. Although some blood products, such as albumin, can be treated to inactivate the agent of serum hepatitis, it is impossible to treat whole blood in such a manner.

Serum hepatitis is much more common in patients who have received multiple blood transfusions, presumably because their chance of being given blood from an infected donor is increased. The disease has led to difficulties in units which perform renal dialysis. Outbreaks have recently occurred in Edinburgh and Liverpool. At Liverpool, 55 cases occurred between March 1966 and January 1971.[7] Another serious risk of serum hepatitis is associated with paid donor services, especially in the United States. For example, one authority found that serum hepatitis developed in 51 per cent of 82 patients given 'commercial' blood but in none of 28 patients receiving blood from volunteer donors.[8] This striking difference is probably related to the characteristics of paid donors in the US, who may include a considerable number of drug addicts and alcoholics, likely to be hepatitis carriers.

The higher risk of serum hepatitis from 'commercial' blood has frequently been used as an argument by those who oppose paid donor services. Until recently, this argument has been difficult to refute, since there was

[5] P. L. Mollison, *Blood Transfusion in Clinical Medicine*, Blackwell Scientific Publications, Oxford and Edinburgh, 4th edn., 1967.

[6] A. J. Zuckerman, *Brit. J. Haemat.*, **19**, 1970, p. 1.

[7] B. J. Hawe, H. J. Goldsmith, and P. O. Jones, *Brit. med. J.*, *i*, 1971, p. 540.

[8] J. H. Walsh, R. H. Purcell, A. G. Morrow, R. M. Chanock and P. J. Schmidt, *J. Amer. med. Ass.*, **211**, 1970, p. 261.

no way of detecting donors who were carriers of the virus. The position has now altered completely with the discovery of the Australia antigen.

Discovery

This is probably the most dramatic and significant advance in blood transfusion in recent years. The antigen was first found by Blumberg in 1964.[9] He was testing sera from haemophiliac patients, who had received numerous blood transfusions, by a process known as immunodiffusion.[10] Subsequent studies showed that the Australia antigen was only rarely present in the serum of healthy people in the United States and Europe (its incidence among the general healthy population of Britain has been found to be in the order of 1 in 1,000), but was considerably more common in apparently healthy subjects from tropical countries, such as Peru, Ghana and South East Asia.[11] Oddly enough, there is no evidence to suggest that there is a higher incidence of serum hepatitis in such countries. A high incidence was also found in patients receiving multiple blood transfusions, in patients suffering from viral hepatitis (20 per cent) and leukaemia (18 per cent) and in certain mentally retarded patients living in large, closed institutions (28 per cent). The association of people in institutions seems definitely to favour the spread of the Australia antigen.[12]

The Australia antigen was finally linked to serum hepatitis by Prince in 1968.[13] He found an antigen in patients developing serum hepatitis after blood transfusion in 8 out of 4,844 volunteer blood donors. He called the antigen SH antigen (SH standing for serum hepatitis), but there is now little doubt that this is identical to the Australia antigen. The antigen is now often designated as the Australia/SH antigen. About the same time, Japanese workers demonstrated a close relationship between the Australia antigen and post-transfusion hepatitis.[14]

A different antigen has been described which appeared to be associated

---

[9] B. S. Blumberg, *Bull. N.Y. Acad. Med.*, **40**, 1964, p. 377.

[10] Different wells in an agar plate are filled with antigen and antibody solutions. The solutions diffuse out into the agar. If antigen reacts with antibody, a line of precipitation forms in the agar between the appropriate wells. When Blumberg put up the haemophiliac sera against the serum of an Australian aborigine, a reaction was noticed due to the presence of an antigen in the aborigine's blood: this phenomenon was called the Australia antigen.

[11] Y. E. Cossart, *Brit. med. Bull.*, **28**, 1972, p. 156.

[12] For example, in a study of over 105,000 blood donations (J. Wallace, G. R. Milne and A. Barr, *Brit. med. J.*, *i*, 1972, p. 663), men prisoners had an incidence of Australia antigen of 1 in 153, whereas non-institutionalised men had an incidence of 1 in 803. A high incidence is also found in patients with long-standing tuberculosis, but not in new patients: this may again reflect the risk of contamination during a prolonged stay in hospital.

[13] A. M. Prince, *Proc. nat. Acad. Sci.* (*Wash*)., **60**, 1968, p. 814.

[14] K. Okochi and S. Murakami, *Vox Sang.*, **15**, 1968, p. 374.

with infective hepatitis.[15] However, this is now thought simply to be an abnormal protein produced when the liver is damaged. A further antigen can be found in the faeces of patients suffering from infective hepatitis: this antigen appears to be related to the Australia antigen.[16]

Incidence

More recent studies have definitely linked the presence of the Australia antigen to outbreaks of serum hepatitis in renal dialysis units. For example, in the Liverpool outbreak referred to earlier, Australia antigen was detected in 7 of 9 staff members with hepatitis and 9 of 17 patients receiving treatment in the unit.[17] The results have now led the Liverpool dialysis unit to introduce routine screening of both patients and staff for Australia antigen before joining the unit.[7] If the test is positive, they are rejected. Blood for priming the dialysis machines or for transfusion will be screened either before transfusion, or immediately afterwards. Ideally, blood will come from Australia antigen negative 'safe' donors, whose blood has been transfused on 10 or more occasions without causing serum hepatitis. By these means, it is hoped to prevent the virus of serum hepatitis from entering a renal dialysis unit. A prospective study of hepatitis in 20 dialysis units in the UK[18] showed that all of the outbreaks were associated with Australia antigen. After patients positive for the Australia antigen were isolated for dialysis, there was a marked fall in the incidence of hepatitis among staff.

A link has also been shown between Australia antigen positive blood donors and the occurrence of post-transfusion serum hepatitis. One study on donor blood positive for the antigen showed that 9 out of 12 recipients transfused with the blood developed serum hepatitis and, in 7 of the 9, the antigen could later be demonstrated.[19] Of 69 patients receiving Australia antigen negative donor blood, only 4 developed hepatitis of some sort or the other, but the antigen could not be detected in them. It is probable that these cases of hepatitis were caused by some other virus.

A study of patients with hepatitis in Liverpool and North Wales[20] showed an incidence of positive tests for Australia antigen in 74 per cent of those with a history of blood transfusion, needle transmission or renal dialysis, and in only 8·3 per cent other patients. There was some evidence to suggest that the occurrence in young adults of hepatitis together with a positive antigen test could sometimes be linked to drug addiction, probably by injection. This finding has been confirmed in the US in areas where

---

[15] S. Del Prete, D. Constantino, M. Doglia, A. Graziina, A. Ajdukiewicz, F. J. Dudley, R. A. Fox and S. Sherlock, *Lancet*, *ii*, 1970, p. 579.

[16] A. A. Ferris, *Brit. med. Bull.*, **28**, 1972, p. 131.

[17] G. C. Turner and G. B. B. White, *Lancet*, *ii*, 1969, p. 121.

[18] S. Polakoff, Y. E. Cossart and H. Tillett, *Brit. med. J.*, *iii*, 1972, p. 94.

[19] D. J. Gocke, H. B. Greenburg and N. B. Kavey, *Lancet*, *ii*, 1969, p. 248.

[20] G. C. Turner, *Brit. J. Hosp. Med.*, **5**, 1971, p. 296.

drug addiction is a major problem: a positive test for Australia antigen was found in 66 per cent of patients with hepatitis occurring after needle transmission, in 58 per cent after transfusion and in 55 per cent with no definite history of transmission.[21] Another report[22] showed that approximately 40 per cent of patients with serum hepatitis had received transfusions of blood or blood products in the six months before their disease. However, in the 10 to 19 and 20 to 29 age groups, only 7·5 and 14·6 per cent respectively gave such a history. A significant percentage of serum hepatitis patients from these age groups admitted to the injection of narcotics! In contrast, a survey in Australia, where drug addiction is uncommon, revealed an incidence of positive tests in only 17 per cent of patients with hepatitis not related to transmission.[23] Recent surveys on large numbers of blood donors show a lower incidence of Australia antigen in unpaid blood donors (e.g. 0·08 per cent in a Scottish study)[12] than in paid donors (e.g. 1·07 to 1·19 per cent in New York).[24]

Nature

It has now been shown that the Australia antigen consists of a virus. It is much easier to isolate this virus if the antigen is treated with antibody. This causes the virus particles to aggregate; such larger bodies can be spun down in a centrifuge and the centrifuged deposit examined under the electron microscope.[25] The virus is seen as small, pleomorphic spherical particles, long tubular forms with periodic cross-striations suggesting a sub-unit structure and large spheroidal structures. Such an appearance is known to exist in some DNA viruses. The virus can also be found in certain blood products, such as fibrinogen, thrombin and anti-haemophilic factor.[26] The presence of the virus is definitely linked to serum hepatitis and the virus can neither be found in normal subjects nor in patients with infective hepatitis. However, opinion has recently come to regard the Australia antigen virus not as the actual infectious agent, but as incomplete virus particles, possibly part of the protein coat of the virus, or as aggregates of protein sub-units.[27, 28] The detection of these particles is certainly the most sensitive test for the presence of the Australia antigen available;

---

21 A. M. Prince, R. L. Hargrove, W. Szmuness, C. E. Cherubin, V. J. Fontana and G. H. Jeffries, *New Engl. J. Med.*, **282**, 1970, p. 987.

22 National Communicable Disease Center, *Hepatitis Surveillance Report*, No. 31, Atlanta, 1970, p. 21.

23 R. A. Hawkes, *Med. J. Aust.*, **2**, 1970, p. 519.

24 C. E. Cherubin & A. M. Prince, *Transfusion*, **11**, 1971, p. 25.

25 J. D. Almeida, A. J. Zuckerman, P. E. Taylor and A. P. Waterson, *Microbios* **2**, 1969, p. 117.

26 A. J. Zuckerman, P. E. Taylor, R. G. Bird and S. M. Russell, *J. clin. Path.*, **24**, 1971, p. 2.

27 A. J. Zuckerman, *Abstr. Hyg.*, **45**, 1970, p. 857.

28 A. J. Zuckerman, P. E. Taylor and R. G. Bird, *Clin. exp. Immunol.*, **7**, 1970, p. 439.

unfortunately, the technique is too elaborate and time-consuming for routine use.

Antibody

One of the most perplexing features in the story of the Australia antigen is the great scarcity of humans whose serum contains a high level of antibody. Normally, one would expect that most patients who were infected with an antigen, either bacterial or viral, would produce an antibody bearing some relation to their resistance to infection. In serum hepatitis, not only is the presence of antibody uncommon, but it appears to bear little relation to host resistance. This has an important practical application, since antibody is required for all the serological tests for Australia antigen. It is probable that, but for the shortage of antibody, widespread screening procedures for the presence of Australia antigen would have been in existence some years ago. Some of the best sources of antibody are haemophiliacs who have received multiple blood transfusions, including a patient in Liverpool who has received over 9,000 units of blood or blood products.[20] Antibody has also been found in Spain in patients with alcoholic cirrhosis of the liver,[29] and can be prepared by immunisation in animals, particularly the guinea-pig.[30] It is therefore reasonable to say that the supply of antibody is constantly improving.

Detection

There are various serological tests for the Australia antigen. As mentioned above, a supply of antibody is essential for these tests, which all rely upon a substance only present in infected donors—the Australia antigen—reacting with the antibody. One test, immunodiffusion, has already been described. Although reliable, it is not very sensitive and, since it takes at least 48 hours for the results to be read, the test is of only limited use if blood is required urgently.

A more sensitive and rapid technique is known as the complement fixation test. This depends on the uptake of a serum component known as complement, if antigen reacts with antibody. If no antigen is present and the reaction does not take place, the complement remains free and can subsequently be detected. The test has the advantage that a quantitative result can be obtained and it is therefore very useful for confirming a positive screening test. Its most serious disadvantage is that it requires more of the scarce antibody than other methods.

One of the most modern serological tests is cross-over electrophoresis,

---

[29] J. Guardia, R. Bacardi, J. M. Hernandez-S and J. M. Martiniz-V, *Lancet*, *ii*, 1970, p. 465.

[30] WHO, *Bull. Wld. Hlth. Org.*, **42**, 1970, p. 957.

devised by Culliford.[31] The technique is rather similar to that of immunodiffusion, but an electric current is applied, with antigen at the cathode and antibody at the anode. The current causes the antigen, which is an alpha $_2$ globulin, to move towards the anode and the antibody, a gamma globulin, to move towards the cathode. There is no unwanted spread in other directions and if the test is positive a readily visible line of precipitation is obtained when the two meet. Cross-over electrophoresis is at least 10 times more sensitive than immunodiffusion methods,[32] being approximately as sensitive as the complement fixation test.[33] It takes only 1½ to 3 hours to carry out and speed is of the utmost importance in blood transfusion work. Until newer and better tests are devised, cross-over electrophoresis is likely to be the ideal screening test for the Australia antigen. Any positive results can subsequently be quantified by the complement fixation test. The advantages and disadvantages of these techniques have been well reviewed by Cossart.[34]

A new development has been the introduction of a test using latex particles coated with antiserum from guinea pigs immunised with Australia antigen.[35] If Australia antigen is present in the test serum, the particles are agglutinated and can be seen by the naked eye. The big advantage of this test is that it is extremely rapid: the result can be read within two minutes. However, a certain number of 'false' positive results have been obtained and it is probable that the test will be further refined before coming into routine use. The test has great potential as a rapid screening procedure.

Clinical significance

Apart from its importance in blood transfusion, detection of the Australia antigen is also of value for the diagnosis of cases of serum hepatitis in the prodromal stage, to distinguish between serum and infective hepatitis, to keep a check on the course of acute serum hepatitis and to detect chronic liver disease when other laboratory findings show only minimal changes.

In the course of serum hepatitis, the antigen is first detectable three or four weeks before the disease is apparent and then persists at least until the appearance of jaundice. It usually disappears 10 to 14 days later, but may persist for a long time in a few patients.

Some patients with chronic liver disease, such as hepatitis of long duration, chronic hepatitis and cirrhosis of the liver, carry the Australia antigen. Patients in whom the tests for Australia antigen are positive, but who show no signs of liver disease on examination by the most sophisticated techniques, are classified as 'healthy virus carriers'.

---

[31] B. J. Culliford, *Nature (Lond.)*, **201**, 1964, p. 1092.

[32] D. J. Gocke and C. Howe, *J. Immunol.*, **104**, 1970, p. 1,031.

[33] G. B. Bruce White, R. M. Lasheen, M. B. Baillie and G. C. Turner, *J. clin. Path.*, **24**, 1971, p. 8.

[34] Y. E. Cossart, *J. clin. Path.*, **24**, 1971, p. 394.

[35] J. M. Leach and B. J. Ruck, *Brit. med. J.*, *iv*, 1971, p. 597.

Other virus diseases

One factor that may complicate the diagnosis of serum hepatitis and which has been recognised only in recent years, is that certain patients may have diseases after transfusion which resemble serum hepatitis but which are caused by other organisms. One important agent is cytomegalovirus, which usually causes a disorder resembling glandular fever, but which may produce jaundice after transfusion. This infection occurs particularly in patients having heart operations with a 'by-pass' machine, who receive large amounts of fresh blood. It has now been shown that the cytomegalovirus does not survive long in blood and the risk of infection is small if 36 hours elapse between donation and transfusion.[36]

Conclusion

It is now possible to test donated blood for the presence of the serum hepatitis virus. Cross-over electrophoresis gives a rapid and simple screening technique. It is being adapted by much of the National Blood Transfusion Service for the examination of donated blood. Two recent reports from the Department of Health and Social Security confirm that testing for the Australia antigen has come into its own. One concentrates on hepatitis and renal dialysis. Included in its recommendations are statements that only blood screened as negative for Australia antigen and antibody should be used and that staff should not be accepted if Australia antigen positive. The other report recommends that Regional Transfusion Centres should start to test all samples of donated blood for Australia antigen and antibody as soon as possible.

There is some evidence that the serum hepatitis virus may occasionally be present in amounts too low to be detected by present techniques.[37] However, since the sera tested in this study had been stored for 15 years there may well have been some alteration in the activity of the antigen. It is probable that the risk of contracting serum hepatitis from Australia antigen negative blood is very low indeed.

It may be pertinent to end by quoting from a review of serum hepatitis:[20]

> 'The prevention of serum hepatitis caused by the transfusion of antigen-positive blood is now an attainable objective. Within the forseeable future it should be possible to test all blood for SH/Australia antigen before transfusion. For as long as this is not possible for administrative or technical reasons such as shortage of detector antiserum, a worthwhile objective is the testing of all new donors to exclude chronic carriers of antigen. In countries such as the USA where use is made of "commercial" donors, priority should clearly be given to testing blood from this source since it is known to carry a high risk.'

[36] J. G. M. Perham, E. O. Caul, P. J. Conway and M. G. Mott, *Brit. J. Haemat.*, **20**, 1971, p. 307.

[37] L. F. Barker, N. R. Shulman, R. Murray, R. J. Hirschman, F. Ratner, W. C. L. Diefenbach and H. M. Geller, *J. Amer. med. Ass.*, **211**, 1970, p. 1,509.

III. HOW CAN BLOOD DONATION BE INCREASED?

How can more blood be obtained to supplement supply for what is likely to be a much increased demand in the future? One method is reduction of wastage (p. 182). The only other means is to increase the number of donations, either by increasing recruitment of voluntary donors or by offering inducements to donors, financial or otherwise. There is some evidence (Table, p. 181) that the number of voluntary donors is unlikely to increase rapidly. Publicity campaigns tend to rally already registered donors and lead to a subsequent dearth of blood later in the year. There remains the question of inducements.

It is probable that many donors would be highly offended by any thought of payment. However, there is no reason at all to modify the voluntary service. The ideal would be an 'inducement' service running in parallel with it. It would be preferable to begin with a pilot study in one region, to ensure that benefits would be real before such a system were generally adopted. This is more or less in line with the recent proposal by the National Academy of Sciences—National Research Council in the US[38] that a large number of studies into the 'blood-service complex' be undertaken, including the effect of paying a donor.

The problem of inducements is not an easy one to solve. At present, voluntary donors receive benefits ranging from the traditional cup of tea and the more recent glass of beer in the National Blood Transfusion Service to the repayment of 'out-of-pocket' and travelling expenses in the Red Cross Donor Service (though some 90 per cent of Red Cross donors never claim the expenses). The collection of badges and medals for multiple donations also has some attraction. It is possible that in the UK, with a strong tradition of voluntary donation, it would be better to avoid direct cash payments. An extension of the Red Cross system of defraying expenses together with a book token, record token or voucher for household goods of an appropriate value would be preferable. This would avoid the danger of anyone trying to make a living from donated blood, although it would be essential in any case to ensure that an 'inducement' system were subject to the same stringent controls on donors, such as regular blood tests and medical examinations, as the present voluntary service.

Little information on the cost of blood in Britain is available, although it is probable that the figures given by Cooper and Culyer[1] are reasonably accurate. A system of inducements is unlikely to add much to these costs.

It has been suggested that the existence of paid blood donors would lower medical ethical standards.[39] Most of these fears stem from the

38 National Academy of Sciences—National Research Council, *An Evaluation of the Utilization of Human Blood Resources in the United States*, Component Therapy Institute, Washington, 1970.

39 E.g. Titmuss, (footnote 2), pp. 163–4.

situation in the US, where medical treatment of any sort is bedevilled by the risk of litigation, although a recent report from that country[38] suggests that commercial blood banks can provide blood quickly and inexpensively and are suspect in the voluntary part of the blood service partly because of this. In the UK, the National Health Service and treatment for private patients have co-existed very reasonably since 1947. Under such circumstances, it hardly seems likely that the morals of doctors would be debased by an 'inducement' system for donors. There are very few instances where freedom of choice and the existence of alternative systems have exerted a deleterious effect.

The adoption of routine screening for the Australia antigen will, of course, remove one of the strongest arguments of opponents of a 'professional' donor system: that paid donor blood carries a much higher risk of serum hepatitis. One must not forget that the risk of serum hepatitis will also be drastically reduced in blood from voluntary donors, particularly since the number of patients receiving multiple transfusions (and therefore in more danger) is steadily increasing. It has been estimated that exclusion of Australia antigen positive donors in 1970 would have prevented approximately 575 cases of serum hepatitis in England and Wales.[40]

One basic point is vital: there must be *no* question of forcing an 'inducement' donor service on the community. Man must remain absolutely free to donate blood voluntarily if he so wishes. However, a system of inducements for those who would prefer it might well help to satisfy the demand for blood in the coming years.

---

[40] W. d'A. Maycock, *Brit. med. Bull.*, **28**, 1972, p. 163.

Index of Authors

Index of Subjects